Praise for **THE WE GEAR**

"*The WE Gear* shows how y⠀   ⠀ᵢth
good teammates. As a Disney⠀   ⠀ᵉry
single Cast Member played theᵢ   ⠀ᵤ ᵗrue
honor to watch the teamwork m   ᵧᵤₑₛₜₛ dreams work!"

—Rosemary Rose
President of FACE Hospitality
Former Vice President of Walt Disney World

"With *The We Gear*, Lance Loya provides the tools (the gear) necessary to make us all better teammates. This book is a must-read for any coach or leader looking to improve the teamwork within their organization."

—Tony Wingen
Head Coach, Carnegie Mellon University Men's Basketball
Chairman of the NABC Committee on Academics

"Lance Loya has done an incredible job of providing simple yet powerful messages to help anyone become a better teammate. If you want to take yourself and your team to the next level, then shift into the *we gear!*"

—Tami Matheny
Author of *The Confident Athlete*
Founder of Refuse2Lose Coaching

"Being a good teammate does not require talent. Lance Loya brings awareness to *good teammate* ideals and challenges us to self-evaluate ourselves through his five keys of A.L.I.V.E. This unique acronym and approach to developing good teammates is inspiring and spot on. Less *me gear*, more *WE GEAR!*"

—Missy West
Co-Director of Beyond the Game Academy
Former Duke University Women's Basketball Standout

THE WE GEAR

THE WE GEAR

How Good Teammates Shift From ME to WE

LANCE LOYA

CAGER HAUS
PUBLISHING

ISBN-13: 978-1-7325505-4-4

www.coachloya.com

Design and publishing by Cager Haus
Edited by Darby O'Shaughnessy
Cover image: © Serz72 Dreamstime.com

Printed in the United States of America

For Laken and Lakota…may you always be good teammates.

CONTENTS

ACKNOWLEDGEMENTS xi

INTRODUCTION 1

CHAPTER 1: THE ME GEAR 7

The Generic Aisle 9

The Damned Obituary 11

Pleasure vs. Happiness 13

Bringing Clarity to Our Choices 14

A *Perk*-olating Philosophy.................................. 16

Darnell the Mover 18

Becoming ALIVE.. 23

Are You a Good Teammate? 25

The Dunning-Kruger Effect............................... 26

The Good Teammate Survey 28

The Talent That Doesn't Require Talent............ 34

CHAPTER 2: ACTIVE 37

Good Teammate Moves...................................... 39

The Shopping Cart Obsession 42

The Disney Picker 44

Three Communication Standards 47

How to Confront a Teambuster 49

The Height of Confrontation 51

Confronting vs. Complaining 53

Barriers to Acting 54

Four Quarter Teammates 56

Getting Out of Our Comfort Zone 59

CHAPTER 3: LOYAL 61

Your Dog or Your Spouse 63

Mama's Bowling Night 64

Prioritizing Means Sacrificing 67

They Don't Form Teams of Their Own 68

No *I Told You So*'s 69

Connections Squelch Alienation 70

The Peanut Butter Experiment 71

Being Loyal to the Loyal 74

The Skill of Getting Along 76

Become that Someone *77*

CHAPTER 4: INVESTED 79

Investment Lessons from the Financial World *80*

Refueling the Raptor 83

What Else Could They Have Done 86

The Beach Radio Thief 87

An Invested Gift 88

Barriers to Being Invested 91

Circling... 92

The Curious Custodian 94

CHAPTER 5: VIRAL...99

Why the Wookie Video Went Viral............................... 100

The *How* is More Intriguing Than the *Why*.................. 102

A Lexicon Hijacking 104

Killer George 105

He Asked for It... 107

The Hawks' Nest Bench Mob... 109

Contributing from the Bench 111

Victory Cake.. 113

Being Viral Means Sharing.. 115

CHAPTER 6: EMPATHETIC..117

Tanner's Totes... 118

Empathy from the Fourth Wall 120

The Influence of *Why?*... 123

Peeling Back the Layers of *Why*.................................... 124

The Reality of Embarrassment 125

The Montel Mantra.. 127

A Signing Blunder.. 129

Mind Your PD-*EQ*s.. 131

The Escape Room Escapade... 133

A Lesson Learned and Applied 135

Project Aristotle Revisted 137

CHAPTER 7: LIFE IN THE WE GEAR **139**

No Magic Required.. 141

The Backseat Savior 143

A Doctor's Dilemma...................................... 146

The Extent of Your Reach................................ 147

APPENDIX **151**

NOTES... **153**

INDEX.. **171**

ABOUT THE AUTHOR **179**

Acknowledgements

Seeing this book through to completion required a total team effort. I am blessed to be surrounded by some pretty darn good teammates and would like to thank them for their help.

I owe a debt of gratitude to many people, but none more so than my wife, Rachel. Her patience, sacrifice, and unwavering support are appreciated more than she will ever know. She wore multiple hats during the writing process (muse, editor, sounding board, taskmaster, publicist, chief encourager, travel coordinator, single parent, etc.) and she wore them all with excellence. This book doesn't happen without her.

To my daughters, Laken and Lakota, thank you for providing me with endless inspiration. I hope one day you understand why teaching you to be good teammates was so important to me. May you always remember to be good teammates and have the energy to carry on the good-teammate mission when I am gone.

I'm deeply grateful to those whose stories are featured in the book, or whom I interviewed, including Morgan (Swalligan) Cypher, Pam Schilling, Kendrick Perkins, Sean Wyatt, Ashley Foss, Darnell "The Mover," Pat Farabaugh, Lieutenant Colonel Russell Badowski, Steve Mersinger, Tom Walter, Jay Garneau at Wake Forest University, Dan Pillari, Gary Kowal at Monmouth University, Mike Burton, Tanner Smith, Lucas McKay, and Jacquelyn Saunders.

I would like to recognize Cindy Davis and Craig Sikurinec for their special assistance. They both graciously shared their ideas and provided me with vital insight about my original manuscript.

Thanks to Sister Eric Marie Setlock, a.k.a. "*That* Nun." She changed my way of seeing the world and gave me a new sense of purpose. Many of the ideas expressed in the pages that follow are the result of her influence on my life.

Thank you to my Good Teammate Factory clients and the online community members who read blogs, like and share posts, and offer invaluable feedback and encouragement. They are the fuel that powers the *Be a Good Teammate* movement.

I wrote most of this book sitting in a Starbucks, sipping on a grande white chocolate mocha. I have a nice home office, but I find the aura of Starbucks to be more conducive to creativity—plus they have great Wi-Fi! Whether the friendly Starbucks baristas realized it or not, they became my teammates. Many thanks.

A big thank you to my brilliant editor, Darby O'Shaughnessy, for her patience. She was fantastic to work with and her talents brought color to my words. (You are a wonderful editor and an even better teammate!)

Finally, I'd like to thank one more significant teammate—you! Thanks for holding this book in your hands and embracing the message. May *The WE Gear* transform your way of thinking and inspire you to be a better teammate. I'd love to hear from you. Go to my website or find me on social media and tell me about your *good teammate moves*.

INTRODUCTION

With just under three minutes to go in the men's basketball semifinal game of the 2016 Summer Olympics, the United States' DeAndre Jordan rebounded Sergio Rodriquez's missed shot. As a result of that rebound, Jordan tied the Olympic record for most rebounds in a game—a significant accomplishment considering the long and storied history of the sport.

The United States would go on to defeat Spain 82-76. That, too, was a significant accomplishment because most critics believed Spain posed the biggest threat to the United States' chances of winning another gold medal.

Spain's roster included multiple NBA players as well as several seasoned international players who had the firepower to match the Americans. Spain dominated France in their previous game, winning 92-67, as compared with the United States who had struggled to beat France in an earlier competition. Jordan and his teammates barely squeaked by with a three-point victory.

After the semifinal win over Spain, sideline reporter Rosalyn Gold-Onwude pulled Jordan aside for a post-game interview. Jordan's interview was a clinic on how to be a good teammate. Despite his significant individual accomplishment and the notable role he played in his team's big win, he repeatedly deflected attention away from himself.

I sat on the couch in my living room watching the televised interview and marveling at Jordan's replies to Gold-Onwude's questions. He came across as humble, which seemed unusual for someone who had just performed a world-class individual feat. I had recorded the game and was so impressed with Jordan that I rewound his interview and watched it again. This time, I paid attention to the words he used.

In the fifty-two second interview, Jordan used fifteen plural first-person pronouns: *us* once, *our* twice, and *we* twelve times. The frequency with which he chose the word *we* instead of *I* caught my attention; he said *we* twelve times!

"*We* really needed it..."

"*We* just got stops..."

"*We* were able to execute our offense..."

Most people don't speak, let alone think, like that. I mean, come on, who really *thinks* or *speaks* that way? A good teammate does.

My wife was sitting in the room when I replayed the video, and I remarked to her that DeAndre Jordan was in "the we gear" in his interview.

The we gear.

That was the first time I used the phrase *the we gear*. Over the course of the next several months, I came to recognize *the we gear* as the perfect way to explain the art of being a good teammate—a subject to whose study, dissection, and understanding I have devoted my life.

As humans, we live our lives in two gears: the *me gear* and the *we gear*. The *me gear* is all about me. What's in it for *me*? How does this benefit *me*? The *me gear* is our default gear and the epicenter of selfishness. Our focus is on ourselves.

Cars with a manual transmission (i.e., a stick shift) aren't nearly as common as they once were. Today, less than three percent of the cars sold in the United States have a manual transmission. In fact, only eighteen percent of licensed American drivers know how to drive a car with a manual transmission. To use what is, in essence, a lost art—shifting gears—to explain the art of being a good teammate seems strange, but the analogy captures exactly how good teammates operate. For those who know how to drive a manual transmission, bear with me while I briefly describe the process:

With an automatic transmission, put the gearshift in "D," and the car goes forward. Put the gearshift in "R," and the car goes backwards. Put the gearshift in "P," and the car stops. (Just don't try to put the gear shift in "P" while the car is still moving, or the "P" won't stand for "Park" but for "Problem" as in a broken transmission.)

With a manual transmission, you must maneuver the gearshift by hand into the appropriate gears. When more power is needed going up a steep hill, downshift into a lower gear. When speed is needed on the highway, upshift into a higher gear. But before shifting gears, drivers must depress the clutch pedal—that mysterious third pedal missing on automatic cars.

When the time comes to shift gears, depress the clutch and choose the appropriate gear. This instant is known as a *clutch moment.*

Humans have clutch moments in their lives, too—stressful occasions that require them to make quick decisions about how they should proceed. When good teammates are faced with clutch moments, they choose to shift into the *we gear.* They make their choice by asking themselves, "What's best for the team?"

- *The WE Gear* is about cultivating the mindset and methods needed to be a better teammate.

- *The WE Gear* will give you the tools to inspire those on your team to be better teammates.

- *The WE Gear* will take you inside the fascinating psyche of a good teammate through touching and sometimes heartbreaking stories.

- *The WE Gear* will equip you with the insight you need to shift the focus of your life from *me* to *we.*

I have discovered that this shift does not happen by accident. This shift is the result of an intentional commitment to five distinct behaviors that I explain using the acronym ALIVE. Together, we will explore the value of these behaviors and how each contributes to the formation of a good teammate—and by "good teammate" I don't mean a passive follower who is content to simply get in line and practice conformity. I mean a person whose actions are defined by the purity of his intentions and by his willingness to put the needs of the team ahead of his own. I refer to individuals whose way of thinking propels the team toward success.

In this context, the term *team* is not limited to a sports team. Your team can be your staff, coworkers, community, family, church, etc. Everybody is part of a team in some capacity, and most belong to more than one team. Ultimately, how effective we are in our team role depends upon our ability to shift our focus from *me* to *we*. If you want to be a better teammate, coach, teacher, employee, boss, spouse, friend, or parent, this book is for you.

So buckle up and get ready to shift gears. Get ready to discover the *we gear*. . .

THE ME GEAR

Selfishness sinks ships: friend*ships*, partner*ships*, relation*ships*, champion*ships*, even leader*ships*. Like an iceberg tearing through the hull of an ocean liner, selfishness will inevitably send all of those *ships* plummeting to the depths of the abyss. *Selfishness sinks ships.*

Have you ever had the displeasure of being on a team with selfish teammates? The experience is miserable.

Selfish teammates are toxic teammates. Selfish teammates are all for one provided they are the one. They don't listen to what you have to say. They don't value your input. They don't care about your thoughts or your needs or those of the team. They only care about themselves and what is best for them.

In pursuit of their agenda, they will undermine authority. They will deceive, manipulate, and betray their fellow teammates. They will take personal credit for achievements that were attained through the work of the group. They will withhold vital information to prevent another teammate from getting ahead of them.

And they will do it all at the expense of their team.

Toxic teammates are *ball hogs, glory hounds,* and *drama queens*. But more than anything, they are **teambusters**. The toxicity they spew busts the team's cohesiveness and prevents even the most talented leader from guiding the group to success.

If the world of group dynamics has one truth, it's that selfish teammates destroy teams. Nobody wants to be part of a busted team that is incapable of teamwork.

Teamwork leads to efficiency. Teamwork leads to synergy. Teamwork leads to productivity. Everybody wants teamwork. *Teamwork makes the dream work.*

Not to disappoint you, but that last expression is a lie.

All right, maybe a lie is a bit dramatic. But at the very least, the statement is misleading because *Teamwork makes the dream work* is part two of the equation. Part one is: *Teammates make the teamwork.*

How do you create good teamwork? You develop good teammates.

In 2012, Google launched a study intended to discover what makes a team effective. The study was aptly named *Project Aristotle*—a tip of the hat to the Greek philosopher's famous quote, "The whole is greater than the sum of its parts." For the project, Google researchers examined 180 "teams" that existed within their company. They conducted interviews and analyzed employee engagement surveys.

After two years of studying the data, they determined that the most effective teams are ultimately comprised of individuals who are aware of and adhere to group norms—

informal rules that dictate behaviors in the group. In other words, effective teams are comprised of individuals who are good teammates. This is no surprise to anyone who has ever been on a team with a teambuster.

Teamwork doesn't happen without good teammates—those individuals who repeatedly choose to shift into the *we gear* and pursue options that are best for their team.

When a team that's made up of incredibly talented players fails to achieve success, usually its talent never made it out of the *me gear*. Selfishness consumed the players. Nothing prevents the team's most talented players from also being the team's most talented teammates.

The Generic Aisle

At one time, every grocery store in America had a generic aisle—an entire section of the store filled with cheap products in no-frills black and white packages. Crackers came in a plain white box labeled CRACKERS in black letters. Toothpaste came in a white tube labeled TOOTHPASTE in the same black, block-style font. The product's name was the descriptor. For consumers looking to save a few cents, the generic brand was the way to go.

But stores no longer have a generic aisle. The concept—basic products sold at a lower price than comparable national brands—still exists, but the no-frills black and white packaging has vanished. Today, retailers employ the concept through their store brands or clever knockoffs like Mountain Lightning instead of Mountain Dew, or Marshmallow Magic instead of Lucky Charms.

The generic brand failed because, to consumers, packaging matters. The store brands that replaced the generic brands included fancy fonts and colorful graphics that have allowed them to yield a higher profit than many of their name-brand counterparts. The *we gear* concept is an enticing way of packaging unselfishness that makes sense to people who are part of a team.

The expression has a certain simplistic catchiness. It's easy to remember. In addition, the *we gear* appeals to our natural human desire to want to belong to something greater than ourselves. But to really understand the *we gear* requires that we first acknowledge the existence of the *me gear* and its relationship to the *we gear*.

The *me gear* is our default gear. It's our de facto behavioral guidance system and the epicenter of selfishness. Being in the *me gear* is easy since in the *me gear*, our sole consideration is ourselves. The effects our choices have on others is never a consideration.

Everybody starts life in the *me gear*. When we are infants, our lives revolve around self-preservation because infants are instinctively trying to survive. They cry because they need food, and they cannot feed themselves, not because they have an ulterior motive to disrupt the tranquility of their mother's life. Infants are in the *me gear* because they need to be in order to survive.

The path to the *we gear* goes through the *me gear*. At some point, our basic human needs are met, and we start to psychologically mature. To have to make the majority of our choices based solely on our need to survive is no longer necessary. We don't have to be selfish anymore. We start to have options.

As we progress towards self-actualization, *clutch moments* begin to emerge. In the ideal team setting, individuals shift their focus from *me* to *we* when they reach this point of psychological maturation. Unfortunately, this shift in focus doesn't always happen.

So many of the afflictions facing our society (*school bullying, domestic violence, the opioid epidemic, broken homes, political shenanigans, sexual misconduct in the workplace, etc.*) come down to people not being good teammates. These afflictions all have something in common: They are the result of individuals remaining in the *me gear*.

The Damned Obituary

The obituary began by mentioning the names of relatives who preceded the deceased in death as well as the names of those whom he left behind. The notice mentioned his hobbies and his place of employment—but then it went in an unexpected direction. At the end of Anthony Swalligan's obituary were two words, conspicuously printed in capital letters: DAMN HEROIN.

On February 23, 2016, twenty-three year old Anthony Swalligan, a bright, good-looking, kindhearted soul, died as a result of a heroin overdose. Anthony was a popular student who had a lot of friends. He was a member of the Bishop McCort Catholic High varsity football and basketball teams. He came from a big, loving, supportive family. His overdose, beyond being a cautionary tale of how the heroin epidemic does not discriminate, offers surprising insight into the art of being a good teammate.

That teambusters are bad people is not necessarily true. Sometimes they're simply individuals who get stuck and can't shift out of the *me gear*. Sometimes they don't even realize they are in the *me gear*.

The words DAMN HEROIN in Anthony Swalligan's obituary caught the community's attention. DAMN HEROIN resonated with readers. A few days after Anthony's death, an op-ed piece appeared in his hometown newspaper, the Johnstown, Pennsylvania *Tribune Democrat*. The piece described how Anthony's mother was insistent that those two words be printed and emphasized in her son's obituary. She wanted others to know what happened and that she was angry. She wanted her son's passing to be a platform for helping others.

Unfortunately, her words didn't have the immediate impact that she had hoped for. Barely a month after her son's obituary was published, a similar obituary for Chad Schilling appeared in the same newspaper. Schilling was an all-state running back at Bishop Carroll High School—the crosstown rival of Anthony Swalligan's high school. Schilling was the newspaper's Player of the Year his senior season. He, too, had overdosed on heroin.

Over the course of the eighteen months following Anthony Swalligan's DAMN HEROIN obituary, a string of former high school athletes from the *Tribune Democrat's* coverage area succumbed to the same fate. Their stories were eerily similar in that the deceased were all well-liked, came from good homes, and, by all accounts, loved—and were loved by—their families.

What kept them from understanding the heartbreak they were causing their families? What kept them from realizing the dangerous path on which they were heading? What kept them from being able to shift out of the *me gear*?

Their addiction. Their addiction crippled their decision-making capacities. They had broken transmissions, and they couldn't shift gears. Addiction locks individuals in the *me gear* and blinds them to their surroundings. Addiction is like driving a car with tinted windows that are so dark that nobody outside can see in, and nobody inside can see out. Under these circumstances, recognizing clutch moments is impossible.

Toxic teammates get stuck in the *me gear* for the same reason that heroin addicts do. Only toxic teammates are not addicted to heroin; they are addicted to selfishness. Toxic teammates cannot escape the euphoric feeling they get from self-indulgence any more than a heroin addict can resist the pleasure that comes from a hit of heroin. A toxic teammate's dependency on self-interest is that strong.

Pleasure vs. Happiness

The *me gear* is about pleasure, whereas the *we gear* is about happiness. The correlation between the ability to be a good teammate and the differences between pleasure and happiness helps explain why some get stuck in the *me gear*.

Dr. Robert Lustig, revered endocrinologist and author of *The Hacking of the American Mind*, identifies seven differences between happiness and pleasure:

1. Pleasure is short-lived; happiness is long-lived.
2. Pleasure is *visceral*; happiness is ethereal.
3. Pleasure is taking; happiness is giving.

4. Pleasure can be achieved with substances; happiness cannot be achieved with substances.
5. Pleasure is experienced alone; happiness is experienced in social groups.
6. The extremes of pleasure all lead to addiction, whether they be substances or behaviors. Yet there's no such thing as being addicted to too much happiness.
7. Pleasure is dopamine; happiness is serotonin.

The last point about dopamine and serotonin is crucial to understanding the *me gear*. Both biochemicals have value, but too much dopamine can lead to addictions and rob us of our happiness. Dopamine can drown serotonin. As Dr. Lustig explains, "The more pleasure we seek, the more *unhappy* we get."

Much like a heroin addict who builds a tolerance that requires more and more heroin to get the "high," toxic teammates chase more and more individual attention. Their pleasure-seeking choices pose a detriment to their team's well-being.

Bringing Clarity to Our Choices

Prevention is easier to manage than addiction. The chemical dependency that comes with addiction clouds an addict's ability to see the heartache he is causing those around him.

I suspect we would see much different results if we could somehow magically go back to the moment just prior to the heroin-filled syringe plunging into the addict's body for the first time. Imagine if we could show the addict all the destruction his choice would bring—à la Ebenezer Scrooge and the Ghost of Christmas Future. With that insight, in an unaltered mental state, would he still proceed with sticking the needle in his vein?

I don't think he would. I think his concern for his family would prevail and prevent him from proceeding. He would successfully shift his thoughts from *me* to *we*.

Me gear addictions can be treated similarly to other addictions—by getting to the root of the problem. This means getting teambusters to see themselves as teammates instead of isolated individuals, and then getting them to understand the ripple effect their choices have on everyone on the team.

Being a good teammate is, at its most elementary level, a matter of perspective. It's seeing yourself as a teammate and not as an isolated individual. It's understanding that *you are part of a team*, and, as such, everything you do impacts somebody else on your team.

The clarity we gain from seeing ourselves from this perspective is what allows us to care about our team. The *me gear* is about caring for ourselves. The *we gear* is about caring for our team.

In my children's book *Be a Good Teammate*, I identify three things that good teammates do: they care, they share, and they listen. Every positive attribute of a good teammate falls into one of these three categories. I originally wrote *Be a Good Teammate* for my pre-school daughters, but the book's message of care, share, and listen transcends age.

I have learned that most people know what they need to do to be a better listener. Most people also know what they need to do to become better at sharing. What people struggle with is trying to figure out how to be better at caring.

A *Perk*-olating Philosophy

One of the most interesting conversations I've had about the art of being a good teammate was with NBA veteran Kendrick Perkins. I interviewed him not long after the publication on SI.com of a *Sports Illustrated* article titled "Oral History: Kendrick Perkins, the NBA's Best Teammate." The article painted an impressive picture of the value he brings to his team on the court—and even more so in the locker room.

Perkins was a common denominator on some of professional basketball's most successful teams of recent years. He played an integral role in the Boston Celtics' 2008 NBA Championship, starting in seventy-eight games. He helped the Oklahoma City Thunder advance to the NBA Finals in 2012 and the Cleveland Cavaliers do the same in 2015 and 2018.

During his career, Perkins played alongside some of the game's biggest names, including LeBron James, Kevin Durant, Russell Westbrook, Kevin Garnett, Paul Pierce, and Ray Allen. The list includes league MVPs and future Hall of Famers.

At six feet, ten inches, Perkins is a big man with a big heart—and an unusual background. He was raised by his maternal grandparents on a farm in southeast Texas. When Kendrick was only eighteen months old, his father left to pursue a professional basketball career in New Zealand and never returned. Three years later, Kendrick's mother was killed in a shooting incident at the beauty salon where she worked. You would expect someone who started life under those circumstances to be resentful if not jaded. However, nothing about Kendrick Perkins suggests that he has ever been either.

Kendrick's grandparents knew little about basketball except that their rather tall grandson seemed to be good at it. They allowed him to be involved in sports, but they kept him grounded by keeping him active in their church.

Perkins was the self-proclaimed "captain" of the altar boys at Our Mother of Mercy Catholic Church until his senior year of high school. By that time, he was ranked as one of the top basketball prospects in the world and had already decided to forgo college and enter the NBA draft. The Memphis Grizzlies selected him with the twenty-seventh pick in the first round of the 2003 NBA draft, but immediately traded him to the Boston Celtics.

Perkins' modest upbringing and the humility he learned from his involvement in his church contributed to his serve-first approach toward being a good teammate. Quite often, individuals with a neglectful upbringing are inclined to also have a *me gear* upbringing because they are focused on survival and acquiring status. They are unable to see a bigger picture. But that wasn't the case with Perkins.

When I spoke with Kendrick, we discussed his upbringing and the influence his coaches and teammates had had on his life and on the formation of his good-teammate mindset. We talked about how he tried to be consistent. Whether his team was winning or losing, whether he was having a good game or a bad game, he made a deliberate effort to consistently be the same person around his teammates.

I wondered if he considered himself to have a "good-teammate superhero power," so I asked him if he thought he was especially gifted at any one aspect of being a good teammate. In response, he described something he had learned early in his career, for which he credits his former Celtics teammate, Kevin Garnett: the ability to lose himself in the team. Kendrick was referring to being able to let go of individual ambition and self-serving motives, and to replace these with team-driven identifiers. He lost his *self* in the team.

The philosophy is ironic because we live in a society where people are always trying to find themselves. Too many people seem to think the path to happiness lies in finding what gives them pleasure. But pleasure does not equate with happiness. Think of the heroin addicts. They found immediate pleasure, but they certainly didn't find happiness.

The key to happiness isn't finding yourself; it's losing yourself—in the team. When you lose yourself in the team, you discover that your purpose in life is to serve the needs of the team. Service leads to purpose. Purpose leads to happiness.

The *me gear* is where you find personal pleasure. The *we gear* is where you find the real treasure—purpose. To experience the treasure of the *we gear*, you must be willing to abandon the allure of the *me gear*.

Darnell the Mover

I enjoy meeting people with a genuine zeal for what they do. Their enthusiasm for life and the pride they take in their craft has little to do with where they work or even with what they are doing. Their zeal is about their attitude.

The first time I experienced this phenomenon, I was sitting in the lobby of a building in Spartanburg, South Carolina, waiting for a meeting to start. The man washing the building's windows was using his spray bottle and squeegee faster than any person I had ever seen. His movements were a blur.

I was certain that his speed would cause him to do a haphazard job, so I casually walked past one of the windows he had finished to inspect his work. I was amazed. No streaks. No missed spots. The window was perfect. The more I watched, the more I realized how meticulous he was with each window. He would spray the glass and make a few rapid passes with his squeegee. Then he would study the window, looking for any smudge he might have missed. If he found a spot, he would wipe it with his rag and then repeat the entire process. He didn't waste time. His expeditious method allowed him to be more diligent than the other window washers.

I stopped looking at the windows and paid closer attention to him. The entire time he worked, he smiled, which was contagious. His love for his craft radiated. He was inspiring. As I glanced around the lobby, I noticed I wasn't the only person watching him. Others were admiring him, and they, too, were smiling. Through his uncommon effort, this window washer was bringing joy into the world.

In Cumberland, Maryland, I had a similar experience watching a busboy at a popular pizzeria noted for its long line of customers waiting to be seated. Like the window washer, the busboy worked with unusual speed. I marveled at how swiftly he cleared the dishes and wiped the tables clean. Because the busboy worked so quickly, the wait time was drastically reduced. The busboy smiled and worked with the same diligence as the window washer. When he finished cleaning the tables, they were immaculate. He was an asset to his employer.

Of all the blogs I've written, none have gotten a more positive response than the one I wrote about *Darnell the Mover*. Darnell is another example of an individual who so enjoys serving others through his work that his enthusiasm is inspiring.

Moving can be a stressful ordeal. Some health experts list moving as third among life's most stressful events, right behind the death of a loved one and a divorce. When my family moved across the country, we experienced that stress firsthand. We were in a moving nightmare—until *Darnell the Mover* came along and changed everything.

We had hired a nationally recognized moving company to pack and transport our belongings. Despite having signed an agreement that listed specific pick-up and delivery dates, the company called and changed those dates several times. Every time the company proposed a change, they reminded us that "technically" we could opt out of the contract if we didn't agree to the change. Because we had made prior arrangements with our realtors, the utility companies, etc., and because we were unlikely to procure another moving company to accommodate our needs sooner than what was being proposed, we reluctantly agreed to the changes.

On the day the company picked up our belongings, our salesman called a couple of hours after the truck pulled out of our driveway to inform me that the company had underestimated the load's weight. If we wanted to proceed with the delivery, we would need to pay additional fees.

Of course, the salesman reiterated that if we didn't agree to the price change, we could "technically" opt out of the contract and the company would return our belongings. I was livid. I felt like they were holding our possessions hostage, but what choice did we have but to pay them? Issues with the realtors, the utility companies, and trying to find another moving company would still remain, so we grudgingly paid the additional costs.

By this point, we were so stressed figuring out the other logistics of our move, that I didn't care what additional fees I had to pay. I just wanted our stuff delivered and to be done with the moving company that I suspected preyed on stressed clients who felt as we did.

We were so excited to finally see the moving truck pull up in front of our new house—even though the delivery did not arrive on the day the company said it would. My excitement faded, however, when I realized that the driver was the only person getting out of the truck. When I asked if he had a crew coming to help, he nonchalantly replied, "Nope, just me and Darnell. He'll be here soon."

Just me and Darnell? I stared at the huge semi parked in front of me, packed with our possessions and shook my head in frustration. *This Darnell character better be built like a Greek god or unloading is going to take forever.*

Twenty minutes later, Darnell arrived. And there was nothing Herculean about him. In fact, the only thing remotely noteworthy about his physical stature was his uncanny resemblance to DJ Jazzy Jeff, Will Smith's wiry sidekick on *The Fresh Prince of Bel-Air.* I had low expectations for Darnell the Mover, but I was soon reminded why we shouldn't judge a book by its cover.

Darnell went to work, repeatedly lifting the heaviest boxes and pieces of furniture with ease. He had a technique where he would sling the boxes on his back and take off—with the same expeditious approach as the window washer and the pizzeria busboy.

Darnell turned out to be a fountain of positivity. As he lugged box after box upstairs, he smiled and whistled. At one point, he paused and looked at my wife with a big grin and said, "Do what you love. Love what you do. And I just love helping people."

What a philosophy!

Until this man came into the mix, our moving experience was a nightmare. But Darnell changed everything. I stopped being angry about the change in pick-up time, the delayed delivery date, and the additional costs. I stopped feeling stressed and began feeling happy. I went from finding a lawyer to sue the moving company for breach of contract to tipping Darnell and the driver extra because I didn't think we'd paid them enough for the quality of their service—all because of Darnell the Mover's positive disposition.

This effect is what people in the *we gear* have on others.

While Darnell and the driver were unloading the truck, a potentially volatile situation did arise. Another delivery truck showed up. We had ordered a few pieces of new furniture from a local store that weren't supposed to be delivered until later in the day, after the moving company had departed. How would the dueling deliveries be resolved?

Had Darnell complained about our lack of coordination and been angered by the inconvenience, it would have been understandable. He and the driver may even have had the right to refuse to cooperate with the furniture company. But that didn't happen. Darnell's response was, "No problem. We just got to all play in the same sandbox. That's all. It'll be all right."

People in the *me gear* don't respond to inconvenient situations like Darnell did. They rush to assign blame and want situations resolved to their benefit. They can't see beyond their own immediate desires. *Me gear* individuals hate being inconvenienced, yet they don't mind inconveniencing others.

Darnell the Mover recognized the clutch moment. He accepted that coordinating with the furniture company would be an inconvenience. But he also realized that keeping the client happy was of greater benefit to his company, which was his team.

Happy clients lead to repeat business. Happy clients lead to referrals. Happy clients lead to increased profits for the company. When Darnell factored these realities into the equation, his determination to deal with the minor inconvenience caused by the new furniture delivery in a way that was best for his team was easy.

Darnell the Mover, the window washer, the pizzeria busboy, and Kendrick Perkins are all examples of good teammates and evidence that individuals willing to shift into the *we gear* are found in all walks of life.

Becoming ALIVE

What is most fascinating about good teammates being the impetus for good teamwork is that anybody can be a good teammate. You don't have to be tall. You don't have to be fast. You don't have to be strong, pretty, handsome, wealthy, or intelligent to be a good teammate. You just have to be ALIVE.

ALIVE is a label with a dual meaning. Literally, ALIVE means that anyone with a pulse can chose to be a good teammate. Earning the distinction has no physical limitations. But ALIVE is also an acronym for *Active, Loyal, Invested, Viral,* and *Empathetic.* These non-team-specific behaviors are the five keys to being a good teammate.

Active is not standing idly by and waiting for something to happen. Active is taking the initiative to do what needs to be done. Active teammates are people of action. They don't turn a blind eye to problems, and they don't abdicate responsibility by accepting defeat with "It is what it is." They act.

Loyal is honoring your commitment. Loyal is prioritizing your teams. Loyal is not abandoning ship as soon as the seas get rough.

Invested is connecting your success to your teammates' success. Few things create stronger bonds between teammates than taking a sincere interest in each other. Invested is knowing the minutiae of your teammates' lives.

Viral is being cognizant of emotional contagion. Viral is understanding the effect your mood has on those around you and how the repercussions of your actions spread through your team. Viral is using your enthusiasm for your team to energize your teammates.

Empathetic is attempting to understand what being your teammate is like. Empathetic is asking *why* before you pass judgment. Empathetic is creating a safe environment for teammates to consider issues from different viewpoints.

Being a good teammate means not focusing on things you can't control. You focus on what you *can* control. The beauty of being an ALIVE teammate is that all five of these behaviors are well within your control. Your ability to effectively practice these behaviors is not dependent upon anything other than your willingness to shift into the *we gear*.

ALIVE behaviors are also learnable. You can be trained to improve at them. You may be naturally gifted at some behaviors more than others, but excelling at all five is within your reach. Best of all, ALIVE behaviors are relevant to any team setting. They can be practiced by any teammate on any team.

Are You a Good Teammate?

Whenever I speak to groups, I often start my presentation by asking the audience the broad question, "Are you a good teammate?" I don't offer any criteria or explain in advance what constitutes being a good teammate. I am just curious to see how they view themselves.

Are you a good teammate? is an interesting question because people—especially those outside of sports—don't usually think of themselves from that standpoint. The label "teammate" is rarely their primary identifier. Consequently, they seldom have well-defined parameters for what it means to be a good teammate. The audience's answers to my question immediately separate them into different groups.

One group raise their hands because they believe they are good teammates. Whether they are or not is unknown at this time, but in their hearts, they honestly believe they are.

Another group raise their hands, but deep down in their hearts, they know they are not good teammates. However, they don't think anybody else knows, and because they don't want anybody else to know that they know, they raise their hands to mask the truth. When individuals in this group raise their hands, they usually look down at the floor to avoid making eye contact with anyone—a telltale sign of guilt.

I wish the audience could see things from my onstage vantage point. When this insincere group raise their hands, those sitting around them roll their eyes. Teammates know when a person is not a good teammate, even when that person thinks they don't know. No one can fake being a good teammate, and no one can conceal his position in the *me gear*.

The third group don't raise their hands. Maybe they're too apathetic to be bothered by the question, or maybe they just don't want to call attention to themselves. Either way, their reluctance to raise their hands is concerning.

Historically, most of the audience will raise their hands. As best as I can tell, they fall into the category who honestly perceive themselves as good teammates. Sometimes I follow my initial question with a rhetorical, "How do you know?"

What basis do the people in the first group have for their answer? What parameters do they have? What makes them think they are good teammates? The reality is that most people don't know what it means to be a good teammate.

The Dunning-Kruger Effect

Research suggests that people are inaccurate when evaluating themselves, and they overestimate their own abilities. This is particularly true with people who have no real understanding of what makes a good teammate. Psychologists refer to this as the Dunning-Kruger effect.

According to research by psychologists David Dunning and Justin Kruger, people who are the least competent in a specific field consistently rate their abilities as exponentially higher than they are because they are ignorant of what it means to be skilled in that field. They are ignorant of their own ignorance—they don't know what they don't know.

People in the *me gear* don't necessarily realize that they are in the *me gear*.

Dunning and Kruger conducted a series of experiments designed to measure how accurately people assess their own prowess in grammar, logic, and humor. Several subsequent studies have been done in areas ranging from driving a car to taking exams to firearm safety. All of these experiments concluded that the least competent individuals in a field tend to grossly overestimate their skills. For example, those who were statistically proven to be bad drivers usually rated themselves as being good drivers.

Dunning and Kruger's original 1999 study, "Unskilled and Unaware of It: How Difficulties in Recognizing One's Own Incompetence Lead to Inflated Self-Assessments," was spurred by a story about the *lemon juice bandit*—a tale that fell under the category of world's dumbest criminals.

On January 5, 1995, McArthur Wheeler robbed a pair of banks in Pittsburgh, Pennsylvania in broad daylight. He was arrested soon after a photo from the bank's surveillance footage appeared on the local news. The portly forty-five-year-old, who didn't wear a mask during the robbery, was shocked when police confronted him with the security camera video. He was reported to have stated in earnest, "But I wore the lemon juice!" Wheeler had operated under the belief that lemon juice could be used as invisible ink, like in spy movies. He explained to the confused police officers that he put lemon juice on his face, so he would be rendered invisible to the security cameras.

Once the police got beyond their initial laughter, they determined that Wheeler was not insane, delusional, or under the influence of drugs or alcohol. He had simply subscribed to a false belief that left him overconfident.

While not every teammate stuck in the *me gear* suffers from the same level of ignorance as McArthur Wheeler arguably did, they share similarities. As the expression goes, *You can't give what you don't have.* On many occasions, teammates in the *me gear* don't understand what defines a good teammate, so they can't give a *we gear* approach toward being a better teammate. Their ignorance can be problematic and can lead to the same kind of misinformed ideas that created the lemon juice debacle.

Of equal concern is that ignorant teammates are not only unable to assess their own abilities, but they are unlikely to provide an accurate assessment of other team members' abilities since they hold them to the same low standards as they hold themselves. In short, teambusters are unlikely to recognize other teambusters.

The Good Teammate Survey

I was working with a team of intercollegiate lacrosse players. Their team was struggling to jell as a unit because the players had misguided ideas about what it meant to be a good teammate. The players failed to appreciate how their individual choices were affecting their teammates.

The coaching staff discussed the issue. They compared the standards of being ALIVE to specific ways players on their team were expected to care, share, and listen. After much debate, they identified five areas where players were falling short. They believed deficiencies in these five areas had the biggest impact on keeping the team from reaching its potential.

Every team has its own problems. For this team, the coaches felt the players weren't dedicating enough time to both their individual skill development and their academic work. They also felt the players were unaware of the effect their choices were having on their teammates. The coaches arranged their thoughts in the form of a survey that they planned to have the players complete. The five statements the players were asked to evaluate were:

1. Consistently puts in daily time, outside of regular team practice time, working on skills, lifting weights, and watching film, to try to improve as an individual player.
2. Gives great effort with academic work, i.e., goes to every class, is always punctual, studies for exams, takes notes, avoids conflicts with instructors, pays attention, and behaves in class.
3. Listens intently to coaches' instructions and makes every effort to implement the instructions that are given with a receptive attitude.
4. Has a consistent, respectful attitude toward all coaches and teammates, and is not moody during team

functions (practices, games, road trips, study halls, meetings, etc.).

5. Does not cause coaches or teammates stress by being involved in problematic off-field incidents.

The coaches first went through the entire roster and evaluated each player by answering either YES or NO as to whether the player met the standard. They then asked each individual player to evaluate himself. Players were informed that their answers would remain confidential and only their coaches would see their responses. To minimize misunderstanding about what they were being asked to evaluate, the players were given an opportunity to ask for clarification on any part of the survey about which they were unsure.

The results were classic Dunning-Kruger effect. The players whom the coaches identified as not meeting the team standard rated themselves as meeting the standard in four of the five statements. The responses to the second statement—*Gives great effort with academic work, i.e., goes to every class, is always punctual, studies for exams, takes notes, avoids conflicts with instructors, pays attention, and behaves in class*—were, in fact, in line with how the coaches rated each player. I suspect the reason for this was because that statement included two absolutes—*every* and *always*.

The rest of the statements depended on the respondent's interpretation of the standard and were thus subjective. For instance, how much film did the player feel he had to watch to be considered as having met the standard? How much extra time did the player have to spend lifting weights or working on his skills? If a player walked onto the field before practice and made a few uninspired, casual passes, did that qualify as putting in extra time working on his skills? To some players, it did.

The coaches regularly witnessed some players doing hours of intense skill work early in the morning and late at night, while others were, as described above, making a few, uninspired, casual passes just before practice officially started. Yet both types of players checked YES to meeting the standard about consistently putting in time to improve as an individual player.

That the players' responses coincided with the coaches' responses on the second statement (*Gives great effort with academic work*) suggested that the players were not being dishonest, but rather, that they were unable to perform an accurate self-assessment because they were naïve about the specifics of the standards their coaches had in mind. If that was the case, the coaches believed that having supporting data available when they confronted their misguided players might be beneficial. Because they thought showing the players that they weren't the only ones who noticed the problem would be helpful, they added another component to the survey.

The coaches asked every player to rate each of his teammates on those same five statements—only this time, the coaches didn't limit the answers to YES or NO. They asked the players to rate compliance to each standard on a scale of one to ten.

A player who was completely compliant was given a ten, and a completely noncompliant player was given a one. Theoretically, every player could receive a perfect score. No average score was expected or anticipated, just degrees of being more or less compliant.

The theory was that use of a sliding scale would make it easier to show each player how lacking his peers perceived him to be in specific categories. A sliding scale would also potentially lead to more productive discussions between the players and coaches when they debriefed. Rather than turn into arguments over whether the player was being compliant, the discussions would more likely focus on examining what the player needed to do to become fully complaint.

For instance, if a player's peers rated him as a six on the first statement about putting in personal time to improve, the ideal conversation would go as follows:

COACH: "What do you think kept you from getting a ten?"

PLAYER: "Well, I do lift weights and I do extra skill work, but I guess I don't really watch any film on my own."

COACH: "Watching film could certainly bring your score up. I bet if you spent an extra thirty minutes watching film, you would see a big difference in how you play and how much your teammates respect your commitment. What about how much time you spend doing extra skill work?"

PLAYER: "I work on my passing every day."

COACH: "I bet if you dedicated thirty minutes to passing drills in the morning before classes and started charting your workouts, you would also see your rating go up."

When the coaches reviewed the completed surveys an unexpected issue appeared with the scoring. Players whom the coaches identified as meeting the good teammate standards provided accurate assessments of their fellow teammates. They gave the coaches exactly the sort of supporting data for which they hoped.

However, the players whom the coaches identified as not meeting the standards—the teambusters—gave high scores to everybody on the team. Their responses skewed the data and prevented the result from being as profound as the coaches knew it was. Clearly the Dunning-Kruger effect was causing the teambusters to be unable to provide a valid assessment of their teammates let alone of themselves.

The coaches decided to apply a ranking algorithm to the responses that they hoped would render the data as enlightening as it should have been. The algorithm was similar to the PageRank algorithm originally used by Google in their Internet search engine.

Search engine optimization (SEO) algorithms are some of the best kept secrets in the world, and they can be difficult to explain. PageRank improves the relevancy of a web search by deciding what links show up at the top of the page for a search query. PageRank is among the primary reasons Google was considered to be superior to many of the other search engines. The algorithm looks at the incoming links to a webpage and at how important those incoming links are. In the BBC documentary *The Secret Rules of Modern Living: Algorithms*, Oxford University mathematics professor Marcus du Sautoy cleverly explains the PageRank algorithm through a simple sports analogy:

Think of the players on a soccer field as webpages and the ball being kicked between the players as web links. If a player gets a lot of passes from the other players, he would receive a higher ranking. Websites will rank higher and show up closer to the top of a Google search query when that webpage has a lot of links coming from other websites.

Another PageRank factor is the source of the links. PageRank gives more weight to a link that is coming from a website that has a higher ranking. Thus, a pass from a popular soccer player is worth more than one from a player who is not as involved in the game.

To make the survey results more applicable, the coaches weighted the players' responses before calculating the results. They identified the players they considered to be the most compliant with the standards. Three players fell into this category. They weren't necessarily better players, but they had a better understanding of the team's standards and of what it meant to be a good teammate.

The coaches multiplied the ratings from those three players by one and a half before compiling the scores and assigning a "good teammate" value to each team member. The result? A clear picture of the issue emerged. Now a definitive distance separated the ratings of the good teammates and the teambusters.

The Talent That Doesn't Require Talent

This book is part discovery and part assessment. It's an opportunity to think about what it means to be a good teammate and to evaluate your teammates and yourself.

The ALIVE standard (*A*ctive, *L*oyal, *I*nvested, *V*iral, and *E*mpathetic) is a way for individuals to gauge how adept each is at being a good teammate. ALIVE also provides a way for team leaders to convey good-teammate criteria to team members. While the five ALIVE behaviors are common to all good teammates, flexibility within these behaviors allows for specific standards to be applied to every team. But if these explicit details are not identified, members of the team will attempt to figure out the standards for themselves.

An unintended benefit from the lacrosse coaches' survey was that taking the survey helped to boost the confidence level of those players who were identified as good teammates. The Dunning-Kruger effect applies not only to incompetent individuals whose confidence in their abilities is inaccurate, but also to those at the opposite end of the spectrum.

Individuals who are considered highly competent in a field tend to underestimate their competence and wrongfully presume that others have the same skills they have. This can lead to *imposter syndrome*, in which people doubt how skilled they actually are.

The survey allowed the coaches to affirm the abilities of the good teammates. In addition, coaches were able to show these teammates that other players also recognized their contributions. Sometimes people in the *we gear* need to be reassured of their selfless position. Reassurance puts them on a pedestal, which becomes a place of self-motivation.

The next chapters focus on precisely what it means to be ALIVE. You will gain further insight into each specific behavior through a variety of real-life examples. You will also discover the symbiotic relationships among the various behaviors.

Being a good teammate is *a talent that doesn't require talent*. As previously discussed, the *we gear* doesn't require a person to possess any explicit physical attributes. But a person can't be a good teammate by having good intentions alone. The talent—the art—of being a good teammate lies in the actions a person takes. The first step in shifting out of the *me gear* is to be ACTIVE.

Active

Over the years, I have visited a lot of schools. With few exceptions, a "pride" sign is prominently displayed near the entrance to the school's gymnasium. The sign boasts about the school's BULLDOG PRIDE or TIGER PRIDE or WARRIOR PRIDE.

I can't tell you how many times I've walked by one of those pride signs only to notice a large weed growing through the sidewalk, or an old candy wrapper lying in the school's hallway. I've often wondered how many of those "proud" people passed by that candy wrapper without bothering to pick it up and throw it in the trash. How many passed by that weed and didn't bother to pull it out?

The candy wrapper and the weed were in plain sight, impossible to miss. Every person who entered the building saw the candy wrapper and the weed and chose not to act. The opportunity was a clutch moment, and no one chose to shift into the *we gear*.

Before proceeding, we should address the significance of this scenario and why it rises to clutch moment status. The sign claims that individuals at that school have pride in their team. If that was so, they wouldn't want anything to tarnish their team's image by giving others a negative opinion of their team. We assume they would be willing to do whatever necessary to substantiate the *pride* they have in their team.

The candy wrapper and the weed suggest apathy, not pride. Their presence keeps the school from appearing pristine and leads us to believe that people at that school don't care about their team or its image as much as they claim. They don't have genuine pride. If they did, the weed wouldn't have grown to be as tall as it has, and the wrapper would have been disposed of. If they are willing to let something as small as a weed or a candy wrapper go unattended, one wonders what else are they letting slide? The candy bar wrapper and the weed matter. They need to be dealt with.

As individuals walked by, confronted with this reality, their reactions varied:

- Some chose not to care.
- Some thought what a shame it was for such eyesores to exist.
- Some complained about the groundskeepers not doing their jobs.
- Some blamed the situation on poor leadership for allowing the blight to happen.

But none acted to remedy the situation. In a fraction of the time it took to form an opinion, shame, complain, or blame, they could have reached down and pulled out the weed. The problem would have been solved.

Good teammates act. They don't worry about whose job it is or whose responsibility it is. They don't worry about how the candy wrapper got there or who is to blame. They don't sit back and hope for a problem to fix itself. They step up and take action.

In this case, a good teammate would look at the candy wrapper and think, "That litter shouldn't be there. It makes our team look bad. It needs to be disposed of. Picking it up and throwing it in the trash is what is best for our team." A good teammate shifts into the *we gear* and follows through with action.

Good Teammate Moves

Many people have good intentions and good ideas, but they don't act on them. Good teammates are adept at following through with action. Their propensity to act is what makes them uncommon.

When my daughters come home from school each day, I ask them the same three questions:

1. What did you eat for lunch?
2. Who did you play with at recess?
3. Did you make any good teammate moves today?

As any parent will attest, to get your children to give you details about their day isn't easy. My daughters and I have come to an agreement that guarantees me answers to at least these three questions. By asking them the same three questions each day, we have established a routine such that they know exactly what to expect when they return from school. Furthermore, my asking these three questions has increased their willingness to share more insights about their lives than I otherwise would be able to elicit.

In the spirit of full disclosure, my first two are easy-to-answer set-up questions to prime the communication pump. My daughters' responses can be of interest, but I don't get excited about them. I am concerned with their answers to the third question: *Did you make any good teammate moves today?*

Good teammate moves are selfless acts made for the benefit of others and for the purpose of helping your team. Sometimes these acts are small, like picking up a stray candy wrapper. Sometimes they're big, like donating a kidney. But they are always done to help the team. Good teammate moves are what move the team forward. They are the actions we take when we shift from *me* to *we*. The earlier story recounting Darnell the Mover's unselfish response to the inconvenience of the other delivery truck is a prime example of a good teammate move. So are the stories about the pizzeria busboy and the window washer.

I am consistently amazed by my daughters' responses to the third question, *Did you make any good teammate moves today?* Sometimes it's hard to fight back tears of pride because I am so touched by what they share. For example, one time my oldest daughter told me that as a reward for winning a spelling contest, she got to pick a prize from her classroom's treasure chest. She said a girl in her class never has crayons of her own and must borrow other kids' crayons, so she picked a box of crayons from the treasure chest and gave it to the girl who didn't have any.

Another time, my youngest daughter came home from school without her winter gloves. When I asked where they were, she said she gave them away. She explained that when her class went outside for recess, a boy who didn't have any gloves was using a pair of old socks as mittens. The other kids were making fun of him, so my daughter gave him her gloves.

Most recently, my daughters have been packing an extra snack each morning when they leave for school. Each student is supposed to bring a snack for the afternoon break. My daughters insist on packing an extra snack "in case somebody in the class forgets theirs."

Who wouldn't want to be a teammate with someone who thinks this way?

In his bestselling book *Purple Cow: Transform Your Business by Becoming Remarkable*, Seth Godin writes, "Remarkable isn't always about changing the biggest machine in your factory. It can be the way you answer the phone, launch a new brand, or price a revision to your software." The expression *good teammate moves* is a *remarkable* way to entice teambusters to act.

I could have asked my daughters, as I initially did:

1. *Were you kind to anybody today?*
2. *Did you help anybody today?*
3. *Did you do any good deeds today?*

But these are generic phrases. I discovered I got much better responses when I used the expression *good teammate moves*. Like the *we gear*, the expression *good teammate moves* has a certain appeal that makes it easier to embrace. People understand what it means to have *good moves*.

Good dancers have good moves. Ballerina's plié, pirouette, and perform arabesques. Their dance moves lead to applause from the audience. The more moves a dancer has, the better the dancer. Good athletes have good moves. Basketball players dribble between their legs and behind their back. They spin, shake, and crossover. Their moves lead to their scoring baskets. The more moves a player has, the better the player.

Scoring baskets and getting applause from the audience are positive outcomes. Basketball players and ballerinas feel good inside when they achieve these positive outcomes. The concept of *good teammate moves* works because it reminds people that they did something positive for their team and that they should feel good inside after they shift into the *we gear*.

The Shopping Cart Obsession

The stories my daughters tell me about their good teammate moves inspire me and cause me to be more aware of my opportunities to make good teammate moves. How little effort is required to make good teammate moves is astounding when compared with how much we benefit from these actions.

The business axiom *targeting the low-hanging* fruit also works for good teammates, as not every move is monumental. Targeting the low-hanging fruit, or pursuing the easiest sales and the easiest clients, is the equivalent of the smaller, simpler good teammate moves. The irony of this strategy is that it builds momentum capable of creating a strong business or team foundation.

As I became more aware of my opportunities to make good teammate moves, I found myself unable to resist plucking that proverbial low-hanging fruit. I decided to concentrate for an entire month on making as many simple good teammate moves as possible. I made a deliberate effort to shift into the *we gear* every time an opportunity presented itself. The experience was enlightening. By the end of the month, I had developed several habits that without doubt made me a better teammate.

One habit I developed has all but turned into an obsession—a good obsession, but an obsession nonetheless. I started noticing how many random shopping carts are left in store parking lots. People don't push them back into the store or into the cart corrals.

Those abandoned carts can do real damage to cars. They can roll free and leave dents in cars or scratch the paint. They're also inconvenient when they land in open parking spaces and prevent someone from pulling into that space. Dented doors and scratched paint jobs lead to higher insurance premiums. Unavailable parking spaces lead to customer frustration and wasted time. To not return carts is lazy and bad for the community. I decided that, if I really thought of my community as a team, I had a responsibility to be a good teammate and to do something about the shopping carts.

From that point, whenever I saw an abandoned cart, I took action. I was going inside anyhow, so I pushed the carts back into the store. Returning a few carts was a minor inconvenience that was good for my team. I couldn't get every abandoned cart, but my "low-hanging fruit" good teammate move reduced the problem. Can you imagine the impact that kind of good teammate move would have if more people took this approach?

Sadly, most people treat the abandoned carts the same way they treat the candy wrapper and the weed. They complain about the person who was too lazy to return the cart to its proper place, or they blame the store's management for not being more diligent in rounding up the stray carts. They criticize the litterer and those who ignored the weed. The complainers, blamers, and criticizers are missing out on an opportunity to shift into the *we gear* and help their team.

The Disney Picker

Walt Disney was famously quoted as saying, "The way to get started is to quit talking and begin doing." This sums up the essence of good teammates shifting into the *we gear* through action. I am a fan of nearly everything Disney, which is fortunate since I live close enough to Walt Disney World that my daughters can watch the Magic Kingdom's nightly fireworks from their bedroom window.

Because we live in proximity, we visit the parks almost weekly. The frequency of our visits has allowed me to see beyond the magical aura of Disney World and note some of the park's operations that go unnoticed by most guests. I have become rather fond of what Disney managers do when they walk through the parks.

Most Disney Cast Members—as the company calls its employees—wear costumes when onstage. *Costumes* is Disney code for uniforms, and *onstage* is Disney's way of differentiating between employees who work inside the park in front of Guests and those who work *backstage* beyond the sight of Guests. (Incidentally, Disney capitalizes Guest and Cast Member as a reminder to everyone of how important they both are.)

Observant guests will occasionally see members of Disney's management team walk through the park. Although they're dressed in business casual instead of costume, you can spot them because they wear their iconic Disney name tag—and they carry a grabber, a long metal stick with a handle and trigger and a claw mechanism used for picking up litter. Cast Members call these grabber tools *pickers*.

Walt Disney was adamant that his park be kept clean; he insisted that "the streets be clean enough to eat off of." He believed that cleanliness would differentiate Disney from its seedy competitors. Hence, *everyone picks up trash* is among the tenets taught at Disney University, the park's orientation and training program.

Seeing the team's leader perform a task as menial as picking up trash reinforces the value the organization places on cleanliness. While picking up trash can be a humbling experience for leaders, their example can be influential and empowering for subordinates. Not every employee will witness a manager picking up a piece of trash during his or her shift, but employees who see a manager walking through the park holding a picker is reminded of the standard: EVERYONE picks up trash.

The long metal stick has become a Disney institution. Many Cast Members begin their careers at Disney as interns before ascending to the ranks of management. Advancing from "swoop and scoop" litter-removal to the earned responsibility of carrying a picker is a rite of passage. Some managers personalize their pickers with nameplates and other meaningful adornments.

I liked the idea of holding an instrument in my hand that cues a call to action—an instrument that reminds me to act and inspires those around me to act. I came to like the idea so much that I bought a grabber tool for my own use.

I do a fair amount of walking around my neighborhood that, besides the obvious health benefits, gives me time to be alone with my thoughts. As I walk, I notice pieces of litter. Litter makes our neighborhood look bad, so when I see litter, I shift into the *we gear* and pick it up. Picking up litter is a good teammate move.

Occasionally the litter is unsanitary and it seems unwise to touch it with my bare hands, so I started taking my grabber tool on my walks. I no longer have to slow down and bend over to pick something up, and I no longer care about something being too unsanitary to touch. Using the grabber tool eliminates that issue while making the task more efficient.

The grabber tool sends my neighbors the message that I care about the cleanliness of our neighborhood, and that I'm doing my part to help keep it clean. I want to inspire them to take the same action.

Is my walking around the neighborhood carrying a grabber tool a little unusual? A little goofy? Sure it is. But I don't care. It's a good teammate move. Sometimes shifting into the *we gear* means having the courage to not care about what others think. The grabber tool is effective and encourages my neighbors—my teammates—to join me in making good teammate moves.

Besides, a rather successful entity located near our neighborhood seems to be doing just fine by performing *"Goofy"* actions.

Three Communication Standards

Obviously good teammates can be active in many ways besides picking up trash and pulling up weeds—although, metaphorically, some of the more impactful actions will involve pulling weeds. These actions will come in the form of eliminating toxicity from your team, which involves speaking out against wrongs.

Knowing when and how to speak up can be challenging and require discipline. Comedian and television personality Craig Ferguson suggests three questions we should ask ourselves before we speak:

1. Does this need to be said?
2. Does this need to be said by me?
3. Does this need to be said by me now?

Ferguson's suggestion is widely circulated on social media and has been cited many times as sound advice. But adhering to his suggestion might not equate to shifting into the *we gear*. Good teammates have three questions of their own that they ask themselves regarding appropriate communication:

1. Is this being said to congratulate?
2. Is this being said to console?
3. Is this being said to confront?

If what teammates have to say doesn't fall into the category of congratulate, console, or confront, they shouldn't say it.

Good teammates are not jealous. They know that drama erodes the team, so they use these three standards of communication to minimize the potential for drama and jealousy to creep into their team's culture. When they speak to congratulate, they demonstrate support for their teammate's achievement. Good teammates understand that when a teammate achieves, the team achieves—which is the primary objective.

Offering congratulations builds rapport among teammates and strengthens their bonds. Acknowledgement shows awareness of the achievement and emphasizes an appreciation for the value the achievement brings to the team.

Complimenting someone is a way to congratulate. A nonverbal high five is another way to communicate congratulations. I like to think of high fives as the currency of good teammates. The more high fives we dish out, the wealthier we are as a teammate. Whenever we say congratulations or give a high five, we convey our willingness to be in the *we gear*.

But what about when bad things happen? When failures happen? When a team member is struggling, good teammates show their support. In those moments, our teammates need us the most.

Maybe our teammate suffered an injury, or lost a loved one, or somehow fell short in an important endeavor. Whatever the situation, our teammate is hurting and needs to be consoled. Our teammates need us to ease their pain and get them back on track. The encouragement we give when we console also conveys our willingness to be in the *we gear*.

When something or someone disrupts the team's culture, good teammates communicate their displeasure and confront the source of the problem. Good teammates confront teambusters. They can't turn a blind eye to the problem and hope it will go away on its own because it won't. The problem will fester, and the toxicity will eventually tear the team apart.

How to Confront a Teambuster

To think of good teammate moves as merely being positive actions is natural, but some of the most important good teammate moves are negative actions—like confronting a teambuster. *How* you choose to confront will factor in the results of your confrontation. Actions may speak louder than words, but choosing the right words and using the right tone are actions, too. *What* is being said can be secondary to *how* it is being said.

When a disruption requires confrontation, good teammates consider their tone, timing, and words. Choosing the appropriate tone, timing and words is crucial to achieving the desired outcome. Good teammates remember three popular confrontation strategies by their connection to food: the sandwich technique, the oreo cookie technique, and the sweet-and-sour technique.

The sandwich technique (positive/negative/positive) involves a positive comment followed by a negative followed by a positive:

POSITIVE: *You're the fastest player on our team.*

NEGATIVE: *You only go half-speed during drills and that keeps us from getting to practice against fast competition. At game time, we're not used to defending speed.*

POSITIVE: *No player in our league is faster than you."*

The problem with the sandwich technique is the 2:1 positive to negative ratio that causes the negative behavior to be overshadowed and disproportionately perceived. The teammate being confronted is likely to fixate on the last thing said, which in this instance is positive. The offending teammate leaves the confrontation with a positive impression that minimizes the problem.

The oreo cookie technique (*negative/positive/negative*) involves a negative comment followed by a positive followed by a negative:

NEGATIVE: *You repeatedly show up late.*

POSITIVE: *No doubt about it; you work extremely hard once you're here.*

NEGATIVE: *But your repeatedly showing up late is causing our training sessions to get off to a slow start.*

The problem with the oreo cookie technique is that teammates may put up a wall if your first comment is negative. They may become defensive and unwilling or unable to hear anything else you have to say after hearing the initial negative statement.

The most effective strategy for confronting teambusters is the sweet-and-sour technique (*positive/negative*). Cite a positive behavior before bringing up the negative. Starting with a positive lets teammates know that you have been paying attention and that you care about them. Recognize their value, and use their egocentricity for the team's benefit:

POSITIVE: *You are by far our most talented player.*

NEGATIVE: *But you have to stop second-guessing the coach behind his back. Right or wrong, it's dividing our team and keeping us from all being on the same page.*

Addressing toxic behavior after recognizing positive behavior makes team members more receptive to hearing your thoughts on the problem. They are more likely to trust you and perceive what you have to say as being sincere. By your ending the confrontation with the negative, they know that addressing their toxicity was your main objective. They understand the importance of the issue and leave the confrontation thinking about the problem.

The Height of Confrontation

How you confront—the words you choose—can make a difference in whether your message comes across the way you intend. But sometimes *where* you confront matters. I am not referring to your geographic location but to your posture and physical position compared with that of the individual you're confronting.

Height can play a role in how a person is perceived. Studies have repeatedly shown that Western societies prefer taller leaders. Taller leaders are viewed as being more powerful and authoritative.

While towering over someone can suggest a position of power and authority, it can also intimidate and threaten—which can trigger an unintended emotional response in your listener and complicate your ability to deliver your message. When confronted, our psychological predispositions to height can kick in and affect the way we receive the message. These predispositions, however, can be artificially manipulated to suit the desired intention.

Those who intend to convey authority position themselves above the individual when they speak. Teachers convey authority by standing while their students sit. Sports coaches do the same when they make their players "take a knee." Positioning oneself above the audience can be accomplished in various ways, like using stairs or other elevated platforms.

Those who intend to convey equality position themselves at eye-level with the individual when speaking. Sit down beside the person. Create an open environment that suggests equality by removing obstacles like desks or tables that may be separating you. This position is effective when you want to collaborate with someone on even terms.

Those whose intent is to convey praise or gratitude position themselves below the individual when speaking. This position communicates respect and reverence while literally and figuratively causing people to feel that they are being looked up to.

These suggestions have exceptions. Great disciplinarians will confirm that putting oneself in a position to convey authority, like standing while the individual with whom you are speaking sits, doesn't necessarily yield the desired outcome.

The same advice holds true for confronting a toxic teammate. Sometimes, to get below the individual you're confronting is more advantageous. Although going low seems counterintuitive, this position sends a psychological message that you need this individual's help. Rather than coming *at* the person as an authority to force compliance, you are coming *to* the person as a teammate seeking that person's help in solving a problem.

This *Jedi mind trick* of sorts is a clever way to get that individual to become involved in solving the problem.

Confronting vs. Complaining

Complaining is not confronting. Complaining and confronting are different.

Complaining is when you bring up a bothersome problem to somebody who cannot do anything about it or who is not directly involved in the problem. Confronting is bringing the issue directly to the person responsible for the toxic behavior, or to the attention of someone who is able to defuse the situation, like a coach or supervisor.

Complaining can result in you becoming more toxic to your team than the issue or person you are complaining about. Complaining is counterproductive and can turn you into a teambuster.

Confrontations don't always have warm fuzzy endings. Confrontations can be volatile. But if toxicity is not confronted, the team will not reach its potential. When a clutch moment that requires you to confront a teambuster arrives, focus on being honest and sincere. Use the most effective strategies at your disposal and view your confrontation as a good teammate move.

Barriers to Acting

Choosing to confront a teambuster is among the most difficult clutch moments any good teammate will face. But a closer look at the reasons that discourage confrontation shows that they aren't as impeding as we think they are. That we imagine impediments are greater than they are affects our ability to act.

Here are four common reasons we choose not to act that are more manageable than we think:

OVERWHELMED: The problem seems too big to tackle. We convince ourselves our seemingly small contribution won't have an impact, so we choose not to act at all. When this happens, start with the low-hanging fruit. Take whatever small action you can and build momentum. That momentum may spawn more creative ideas and generate more energy than you thought possible—and it may also spark someone else to join you. Soon you won't be the only one attacking the problem, and the problem won't seem nearly as overwhelming.

OVERTHOUGHT: We let our indecision immobilize us. "Paralysis by analysis" can be a real barrier to acting. To want to have the perfect solution before proceeding is natural. Unfortunately, while we're waiting to come up with the perfect solution, the toxicity continues to fester and infect the team. Take solace in knowing that a teammate's first action is rarely the perfect solution. Don't be afraid to just act. Evaluate your progress as you go and make the necessary adjustments.

OVERWORKED: To make ourselves appear unavailable to act is easy. We mistake busyness for business. We pack our days with trivial work like answering email and organizing files, and we convince ourselves that we don't have time to act on confronting a teambuster. We've masked procrastination as productivity. Examine your daily routine. You'll find ways to be more efficient with your time management, and you'll also find that acting on what really matters creates more time than you would have had without acting.

OVERINVOLVED: The easiest barrier to get beyond may be your thinking it doesn't concern you, and therefore you don't want to get involved. Remember: *What's good for the team is good for you.* If the team has a need, then you have a responsibility to get involved. You cannot allow your choices to be swayed by the opinions of outsiders. Don't worry about what others think of your actions. Focus on the needs of your team.

When my daughters were younger, we sent them to day care. They came home one day repeating something the day care staff were saying to them: *You get what you get, and you don't get upset.* In other words, accept what you get and make the most of it.

I understand why the adults told the children this, but I always found the phrase to be unsettling. I put it in the same category as adults telling children: *Worry about yourselves.* Both phrases unintentionally send the wrong message to children.

These phrases encourage children to focus on themselves and not get involved in the affairs of others. But when the affairs of our teammates disrupt the team's harmony, we have an obligation to get involved. Shifting into the *we gear* means worrying about *more* than just ourselves. We *should* get upset by teambusters' toxic behavior, and we should not accept it.

When trying to get someone to be a better teammate, undoing the damage caused by believing that we should accept what we get and only worry about ourselves may be necessary. These beliefs may have been ingrained in people's thinking since they were small children. Being aware of this situation allows good teammates to be less frustrated and more effective in attacking the problem.

Four Quarter Teammates

To be a good teammate, how many good teammate moves does a person need to make?

A basketball coach was trying to motivate his team before a big game by going around the locker room and asking each player what his goal was for the game.

The coach asked the team's leading scorer, "How many points are you going to score tonight?"

The player declared, "I'm going to score forty points tonight!"

The coach asked the team's point guard, "How many assists are you going to have tonight?"

The player responded with even more enthusiasm, "I'm going to dish out ten assists!"

The coach asked the team's best defender, "How many steals are you going to get tonight?"

The player screamed, "I'm going to get ten steals tonight!"

Then the coach looked at the team's best rebounder. "How many rebounds are you going to get tonight?"

The player calmly stated, "All of them."

To want to quantify our ambition is natural, so we try to set measurable goals for ourselves. However, the matter-of-factness of the last player's response more accurately captures how someone who's shifted into the *we gear* thinks.

The player doesn't know how many rebounds he is going get. He may get one. He may get ten. He may get fifty. What he does know is that he is committed to putting his best effort into getting every rebound possible. He intends to get them all. How many good teammate moves does a good teammate *try* to make? *All of them.*

In the beginning, an aspiring good teammate may not be aware of how many opportunities exist to make good teammate moves. In a common human resources training exercise, managers are advised to put ten pennies in their pocket. Each time they have a positive interaction with an employee, the managers are supposed to move one of the pennies to their other pocket. The goal is to move all of the pennies to the other pocket by the end of the work day. (I have heard of teachers engaging in the same exercise each time they say something kind to a student.)

Since aspiring good teammates can be easily discouraged when they start out, I advise them to be *four-quarter teammates*. The basic principle is the same as the pennies exercise, only instead of the ten pennies, they use four quarters—which is also a play on words.

Coaches get frustrated when players slack off and don't give their best effort throughout the entire game. Some players start the first quarter fired up, but their efforts wane as the game progresses, letting the opponent get back into the game and potentially mount a comeback. Other players start slowly and try to turn "it" on in the fourth quarter. By that point, the damage is already done and the deficit is too large to overcome. The optimal scenario is for players to consistently give their best effort through all four quarters of the game.

The logic behind advising aspiring good teammates to be four-quarter teammates is that making just four good teammate moves is easily attainable and will cause them to be more aware of the low-hanging fruit while giving them a firm base. Over time, they will become addicted to the positive feeling that comes from making a good teammate move. They will grow in tune with the abundance of good teammate moves available, and, before long, they will be going after *all of them*.

Getting Out of Our Comfort Zone

The best way to get teammates to become active and make good teammate moves is to recognize and reward players who make them. Good leaders know how to encourage others, but the best leaders create an environment where team members are self-motivated and able to recognize and reward themselves. The *four-quarter teammates* exercise is a way to get players to shift their focus from *me* to *we* and to become self-motivated.

We like feeling inspired, and we don't like feeling frustrated. Taking action—particularly if it involves confrontation—can take us out of our comfort zone and cause us to become frustrated. We see our reward for choosing *not* to confront as our being able to remain in our comfort zone and avoid frustration. But if we step back and see the bigger picture, we will realize that staying in our comfort zone isn't as rewarding or beneficial as we believed it to be.

Clutch moments where we choose to shift into the *we gear* can force us outside our comfort zone. When this happens, it is important to remind ourselves that the frustration caused by the shift is temporary and that bigger and better benefits will result.

At times a player must set aside pride, like when a senior athlete has to get a cup of water for a freshman who is playing in front of him. The action is humbling and maybe frustrating, but it's the action that is best for the team in that moment. Ensuring that the freshman player is adequately hydrated gives the team a better chance to achieve.

Taking action that forces us out of our comfort zone is a way we learn. As an ancillary benefit, trial and error allows us to acquire knowledge that can be used to our team's advantage. Knowledge is meant to be shared, not stored. Good teammates don't keep things they've learned to themselves; they share them with the other team members—even if sharing that information gives another teammate an advantage. That's part of living life in the *we gear*.

Before we can *LIVE*, however, we must be *ACTIVE*. Actions demonstrate a person's commitment to the other four behaviors (*L*oyal, *I*nvested, *V*iral, and *E*mpathetic). The symbiotic relationship between *ACTIVE* and the other four behaviors is that the other four behaviors are the reasons we act.

LOYAL

How does being loyal lead a good teammate to act?

In 2013, the National Basketball Association instituted the Twyman-Stokes Teammate of the Year Award to recognize the league player who best embodies the characteristics of the ideal teammate. Unlike the NBA's Most Valuable Player Award, which is chosen by a panel of media, the Twyman-Stokes Award is voted on by the players.

Jack Twyman and Maurice Stokes, for whom the award is named, were Cincinnati Royals (Sacramento Kings) teammates. Their fascinating story shows that the NBA could not have chosen more worthy namesakes for the award.

Standing 6-foot-7 and weighing 260 pounds, Stokes was a physical marvel. He was the most versatile and athletically-gifted player of his generation. As a big man, he could not only rebound, but he could shoot, handle the ball, run the floor, and pass as well as any guard in the league. His game was ahead of its time. Legendary Boston Celtics coach Red

Auerbach compared him to Magic Johnson saying Stokes was "one of the few guys that could play five positions." In the book *Tall Tales: The Glory Years of the NBA, in the Words of the Men Who Played, Coached, and Built Pro Basketball*, author Terry Pluto described Stokes as the NBA's "first black star."

Following a stellar four-years at tiny Saint Francis College in Loretto, Pennsylvania, where he was named an All-American and the MVP of the prestigious National Invitational Tournament, Stokes began a promising professional basketball career. He was honored as the NBA's Rookie of the Year in 1957 and set a record for single-season rebounds in 1958. He seemed destined to become one of the game's all-time greats.

But the trajectory of Stokes' career was forever altered in the spring of 1958 when, during his team's final regular season game against the Minneapolis Lakers, he was knocked unconscious after an awkward fall. Three days later, complications related to that fall left Stokes permanently paralyzed.

Professional athletes of that era were not afforded the kind of medical and financial support that today's athletes enjoy. The Royals cut the three-time all-star shortly after his injury, leaving him without a pension plan and without any income. When Stokes' family was unable to cover his mounting medical bills, Twyman became his teammate's legal guardian and assumed full responsibility for Stokes' care.

Twyman organized numerous charity events to raise funds for Stokes. On Stokes behalf, he successfully sued the State of Ohio in one of the NBA's first-ever workers compensation claims. Twyman additionally spent hundreds of hours visiting with his teammate in the hospital. Their bond became legendary, transcending their different races and social backgrounds.

What Jack Twyman did for Maurice Stokes was incredibly generous and a *good teammate move* of epic proportions. His action was the sort that offers a glimpse into the way good teammates view loyalty. Good teammates do not subscribe to the idea that loyalty is a two-way street. Twyman didn't help his teammate because he thought he would get something in exchange for his efforts. Stokes was paralyzed, broke, and had nothing concrete to offer. Twyman helped his teammate because he believed that helping Stokes was the right thing to do.

Twyman's loyalty to Stokes stemmed from his commitment to his belief that for good teammates, loyalty is something you give regardless of what you get back. Good teammates don't expect a payback. They don't think of loyalty as being a conditional transaction: *If I do _____ for you, then you will do _____ for me.* The same applies to the logic of *I've got your back and you've got mine.* These ways of thinking aren't loyalty; they're bartering.

Good teammates view loyalty as a gift. They give without expectation of getting back. They are loyal because they believe in what they are supporting. They've *got your back* regardless of whether you've got theirs.

Your Dog or Your Spouse

An old a tongue-in-cheek hypothetical question is often posed when people want to explain a dog's loyalty: If you locked your dog and your spouse in the trunk of your car and drove around for an hour, which one would greet you with affection when you opened the trunk?

Obviously, the answer is your dog. That comical illustration—viewed from the dog's perspective—conveys the uncommon loyalty good teammates have to their team. They don't abandon ship when the seas get rough. They weather the storm. They are *fully* committed to honoring their commitment.

To be prepared to shift into the *we gear* when clutch moments arise, you cannot pick and choose when to be loyal. You need to stand by your commitment and remain faithful to your team. Loyalty must constantly be at the forefront of your decisions. Loyalty must be about you and not about the other person's response.

Most individuals stay true to their team as long as the sailing is smooth and they are benefiting from the relationship—i.e., the team is winning. But what happens when individuals stop benefiting or when adversity strikes? Teamwork breaks down. Individuals revert to self-preservation and stop engaging in actions that lead to teamwork.

Teamwork may break down, but good teammates don't. They don't break down because of their perspective on loyalty. Remember: When you focus on building the teammate, teamwork takes care of itself. Good teamwork is sustained through the loyalty of good teammates.

Mama's Bowling Night

I worked with a kind and friendly woman who loved bowling. Everybody in our office adored her. The closest she had to an actual character flaw was her unusual obsession with bowling. She absolutely loved to go bowling.

Every Wednesday, she participated in a competitive bowling league. She was unapologetic in planning her life around that league. She even avoided activities like typing on her keyboard on Wednesday afternoons so her wrist could be "rested" for bowling that night.

The woman had a cute and precocious daughter who happened to appreciate her mother's bowling obsession better than anyone. At the time, I was coaching a team whose games were scheduled for Wednesday nights. One day I asked the daughter if she was going to come to my team's next game.

"I can't. It's Mama's bowling night." Her priceless response made everyone laugh.

Mama's bowling night became our running joke. Every time I saw the daughter, I would attempt to entice her with some sort of reward if she would come to the game. Every time she declined, and every time I upped the ante.

I offered to take her for ice cream if she came to the game.

"I can't. It's Mama's bowling night."

I offered to take her to Chuck E. Cheese if she came to the game.

"I can't. It's Mama's bowling night."

I offered to buy her an iPad if she came to the game.

"I can't. It's Mama's bowling night.

I even jokingly offered to take her to Disney World if she came to the game.

"I can't. It's Mama's bowling night.

No matter how ridiculous my offer was, she remained steadfast: *I can't. It's Mama's bowling night.* Because her mother loved bowling, decisions in their family revolved around *Mama's bowling night.*

The woman eventually moved on to a different job, and I no longer saw her daily. Several years later, however, I bumped into her and asked about her bowling escapades.

"I don't go bowling anymore. I gave it up." I was shocked! I could not imagine her having willingly given up bowling.

The woman went on to explain how her daughter—now a fourth grader—was struggling with math. Her daughter's math teacher gave the class a quiz every Thursday. The students had to pass the quiz, or they didn't get the bonus of extra recess on Friday. The students who failed the quiz remained in the classroom for supplemental tutoring while everyone else got to go to the playground. Because the woman didn't want her daughter to miss out on the extra recess, she spent Wednesday nights prepping her daughter for the quizzes instead of going bowling,

This was a clutch moment for the mother, and she chose to shift into the *we gear.* Her choice represents an essential element of being loyal—being able to prioritize teams. In reality, we likely belong to multiple teams in our lives. At times our commitments will create conflicts between two of our teams. The mother loved to bowl and have fun with her bowling team. But she also had a commitment to her other team—her family. In this case, her commitment to her daughter's education took precedence over her love for bowling.

The choice seems natural, but many bring turmoil into their lives because they are unable to prioritize their teams. Good teammates don't have this problem. They know where their loyalty lies, and they establish a clear hierarchy as to which teams get the greater commitment.

Prioritizing Means Sacrificing

Failure to establish measures that prioritize your teams leads to conflict. Imagine scheduling a meeting for your department in your building's main conference room, only to discover that another group needs that room for its function. For example, it's Administrative Professionals Day and someone has dropped the ball. Those responsible forgot to plan an event for these valued staff members, and the best place to hold their last-minute luncheon is the main conference room that you have reserved.

You did your due diligence and checked the availability of the room weeks ago. You went through the proper channels and filed the correct paperwork to reserve the room, which is also the ideal location for your meeting. Furthermore, you put a lot of time into preparing for the meeting. The mistake was not your fault. How do you handle this conflict? Do you put up a fight for your claim to the room? Do you appeal to a higher authority? Do you pout?

Because good teammates can prioritize their teams, they respond by considering the best interests of the organization and not just those of their specific department. They realize their department is only part of the team. They also realize and understand the significance of Administrative Professionals Day. These staff members perform important work and play a vital role in the functioning of the organization. Recognizing their contribution to the team on that particular day is important.

Can you move your meeting to a different day? Can you change your meeting to a different time? Can you hold your meeting in a less-than-ideal location? Most importantly, can you make any of those concessions without being resentful or without causing a rift in your team?

Good teammates can.

They Don't Form Teams of Their Own

The beauty of the *Good Teammate* message is that it transcends age. Groups ranging from elementary students to retirees respond to the message. In fact, one of the most interesting groups to whom I ever presented was foster grandparents.

The Foster Grandparent Program is a Senior Corps national service initiative that allows older volunteers an opportunity to use their life experience to benefit children in their local communities. The program was established in 1965 and was originally intended to showcase the unique ability older persons have to make personal connections with children with special needs.

Today over 350 Foster Grandparent Programs in the United States with more than 35,000 Foster Grandparent volunteers serve as role models, mentors, and friends to children in daycare centers, schools, and various youth facilities. Foster Grandparents are thoughtful, generous people who provide a wonderful service to their communities.

At first I questioned why a group comprised of such goodhearted people needed to hear a message about being good teammates. When I inquired, the director of the program didn't mince words. "We have a clique problem." If the first rule of good teammate loyalty is *Loyalty is not a two-way street*, the second rule is *Good teammates don't form teams of their own.*

Cliques are mini-teams within the bigger team that destroy bigger teams from the inside out. Cliques lead to factions and bullying. They lead to ulterior agendas. The origin of broken teams can usually be traced to the formation of cliques.

You can avoid being drawn into cliques by becoming aware of how they start. For example, someone on the team becomes dissatisfied. That individual is too cowardly to express his or her displeasure in front of the entire team, so he or she starts putting out feelers, fishing for other malcontents. The conversation begins with noncommittal questions like, "What do you think of the new policy?" or "What are your thoughts about the boss's decision?"

If the dissatisfied team member gets an opposing response, the conversation goes no further. But if the person picks up on a hint of shared dissatisfaction, the flood gates open. The negativity starts to spew, and the clique is born.

When the conversation takes a negative tone, good teammates shift into the *we gear* and become tone deaf. They don't engage in negativity.

No *I Told You So*'s

By adhering to a few simple practices, cliques can be disposed of before they start to take root. If you disagree with a team decision, be open about your opposition. Let your teammates know how you feel. Be vocal. Raise your objections. Offer alternative suggestions. But voice your concerns before the decision is made. Once the decision has been made, let your objections go. Get on board and put all your effort into making the decision successful.

Individuals in the *me gear* who don't get their way try to undermine the decision. They either don't put forth the necessary effort to make the decision a success, or they sit back and allow it to fail— and when it fails, they cannot wait to bring up their previous objections and say *I told you so.*

Good teammates don't believe in *I told you so's.* Their loyalty keeps them from making such unconstructive responses. After a team decision is made, they don't waste time naysaying because they are too devoted to finding a way to make the decision work. Should the decision happen to fail, good teammates take ownership of the failure as if they had come up with the idea in the first place. They don't distance themselves from the failure; they own it.

Good teammates suppress cliques by not getting involved in gossip. Talking behind a teammate's back and spreading half-truths is a surefire way to divide your team because gossip forces teammates to pick sides. When someone shares a juicy bit of gossip, your loyalty must be to your team. That means you either relay what you've heard directly to the teammate concerned, or you keep it to yourself. You do not share it with another teammate. A divided team defeats itself.

Good teammates further try to dissuade the gossiper from continuing to spread gossip.

Connections Squelch Alienation

Not every clique is a product of malcontent. In the case of the Foster Grandparent Program, some of the cliques developed from the volunteers not wanting to venture outside of their comfort zones. They only wanted to interact with those with whom they were already friends. They weren't embracing the diversity of the organization.

Cliques formed from this situation result in alienation. People start to feel isolated and no longer part of the team. By not attempting to interact with those outside their clique, they stunt the productivity of the organization, which leads to an *unconnected* team.

Good teammates make themselves available to everybody on the team. They deliberately try to connect with different members of the team on a regular basis. Their efforts to make multiple connections strengthen the bond between them and their teammates.

An admirable quality of good teammates is a willingness to stand up for those who cannot stand up for themselves. If teammates confine themselves to those who reside within their clique, they limit the impact they can have on the entire team. Other members who could benefit from their connection may be outside their clique.

Cliques that cause alienation can lead to bullying. Individuals in the clique begin to view themselves as exclusive. Those not in the clique are subjected to unwelcomed ridicule and can feel ostracized, which will lead them to seek inclusion elsewhere where they'll probably form their own clique. More cliques translate into greater divisions within the team.

The Peanut Butter Experiment

George W. Jenkins opened his first Publix store on September 6, 1930. If you've spent time in the southeastern

United States, you are familiar with Publix Super Markets. They are unbelievably popular, and they are everywhere. Publix Super Markets were founded on the virtue of loyalty.

Jenkins began working as a stock boy at a Piggly Wiggly grocery store in Winter Haven, Florida at the age of seventeen. He quickly worked his way up to become the successful store's manager, but he quit after an unpleasant encounter with Piggly Wiggly's new corporate owners.

Allegedly Jenkins was denied even a short face-to-face meeting with the Atlanta-based owners, despite his having driven more than eight hours to see them. They were said to have been too busy to meet with him. But while Jenkins waited outside their office, he overheard the new owners talking about golf. In that moment, he vowed to return to Winter Haven and open a rival store that treated its employees with respect.

Today, with nearly 1,200 stores and roughly 190,000 employees, Publix is the largest employee-owned grocery chain in America. Even though the company does more than $34 billion in annual sales, it remains true to Jenkins' original pledge to treat employees and customers like family—a commitment substantiated by Publix's twenty-two consecutive years on *Fortune* magazine's *100 Best Companies to Work For*. Publix is one of only eight companies to have made the list every year it has been published.

Publix built its reputation on superior customer service. The first time I experienced Publix customer service, I was in the checkout line, and because nobody was available to bag my groceries, I started bagging them myself. Bagging groceries didn't seem like a big deal to me. Standing nearby were two men wearing suits and ties who appeared to be involved in an important conversation. They stopped talking, rushed to my checkout line, and took over bagging my groceries.

I learned they were regional managers in the middle of a store visit. Baggers are a thing of the past at many large grocery stores, but not at Publix. Bagging is a service Publix is still committed to providing for their customers.

I was impressed with the managers' willingness to humble themselves to perform such a menial task as bagging groceries. I told them, and then relayed an incident I had witnessed in their store earlier that day.

I described how I had been walking down an aisle when an elderly man approached an employee who was busy stocking shelves. The man told the employee he couldn't find the peanut butter. The employee immediately put down the boxes in his arms and took the man to where the peanut butter was located. I found that to be an example of extraordinary customer service.

I would have expected the employee to respond, "The peanut butter is in aisle seven" or "The peanut butter is by the bread." To many, either response would have shown sufficient courtesy. But at Publix, where employees practice *superior* courtesy, I learned that physically escorting customers to the item is standard procedure.

My ever-present *good teammate* curiosity got the best of me, so I asked the managers if they hired employees who were naturally helpful or if they trained their employees to be that way. They smiled and replied, "Both."

Over the next several months, because I wondered how consistent Publix employees were in their approach to helping customers find items, I visited different Publix stores, each time seeking out a busy employee to ask where I could find the peanut butter. Without exception, the employee graciously walked me to the peanut butter aisle and pointed directly to the jars.

Not only was I amazed by the employees' consistency, but I was impressed that the employees who made that extra effort to walk me to the item made me feel special and valued—even though peanut butter, a common item, is sold in every grocery store in America and should be easy to find.

In fairness, peanut butter was easy to find at Publix. But although the jars were never hidden away in an unusual location, none of the Publix employees made me feel stupid for not being able to find my item. Their response showed their loyalty to their customers—and increased my loyalty to them.

Whenever Publix employees walk customers to an item's location, they are shifting into the *we gear*. They are solidifying their loyalty to their team by showing that they understand the ramifications of their actions. Customers who leave the store frustrated because they can't find an item aren't likely to become repeat customers. The employees' compassionate response creates loyal customers.

Good teammates know that loyal customers do the company's marketing for it. Loyal customers share their positive experiences with others. Good word of mouth is a proven way for companies to grow their customer base.

Being Loyal to the Loyal

New customers don't generate nearly as much revenue as returning customers, which is one reason companies so badly crave loyal customers and why companies strive to secure them. Additionally, the buzz created by a loyal following drives new customers to join the frenzy.

Companies scramble to convert new customers into loyal customers. They take advantage of our innate human desire to want to belong by offering promotions and enrollment in loyalty programs. If we buy ten cups of coffee, our next cup is free. Or if we spend $50, we get 5,000 reward points.

According to the COLLOQUY Loyalty Census, the average American household has memberships in at least twenty-nine different loyalty programs. While the effectiveness of these loyalty programs is debatable, their prevalence in the marketplace is not. It's worth noting that a company like Publix—that has high customer loyalty—does not have a loyalty program. Publix relies on its selection of quality products and its guarantee of superior service to maintain its loyal customer base. By all indications, their strategy works.

Publix demonstrates a great irony of loyalty: When you concentrate on being consistent and stop focusing on what you get in return for your loyalty, people become loyal to you. This irony regularly happens to good teammates.

Good teammates are not moody. They are predictable. We know what to expect from them, and their consistency is what allows us to trust them. Because they concentrate on being consistent in their actions, good teammates generate that aspect of loyalty that most individuals mistakenly expect—reciprocated commitment. People become loyal to the loyal, and the *loyalty boomerang* always seems to mysteriously come back to them.

The Skill of Getting Along

Karam Chand passed away on September 27, 2016. His death brought an end to what was believed to have been the longest marriage in recorded history. Karam and his wife Kartari were married for a total of 90 years and 291 days. If ever there was a marriage built on loyalty, that marriage was the Chands'.

Karam grew up on a farm in Panjab, India when the country was still part of the British empire. In 1925, he wed Kartari though an arranged marriage in a traditional Sikh ceremony. The couple moved their family to Bradford, England in 1965. Together, they welcomed into the world eight children, twenty-seven grandchildren, and dozens of great grandchildren.

In an interview for their ninetieth anniversary, the Chands told BBC News that the secret to their long marriage was that they never argued. Kartari was quoted in *The Daily Mail* as saying, "We just get along with each other, and we are family focused. It's simple really."

As the saying goes, if love is blind, marriage is an eye-opener. Anyone who has been married can attest to the truth to this belief. Being committed to a relationship tests our resiliency. For the Chands to credit the success of their marriage to being family (team) focused and to getting along testifies to their willingness to be good teammates.

The *ability to get along* is a skill that frequently goes unrecognized because we don't think of it as a skill. But *the ability to get along* certainly is a skill—a skill that good teammates have. Being able to get along is being able to control your contempt for what annoys you while doing your best to not annoy your teammates. Being able to get along is trying to not inconvenience any of your teammates, but not minding should they inconvenience you. The ability to get along is strengthened by the ability to be loyal.

Become that Someone

This chapter began by my referencing the relationship between Maurice Stokes and Jack Twyman—the namesakes of the NBA Teammate of the Year Award. I described Stokes' physical attributes and mentioned his impressive awards. I would be remiss if I didn't do the same for Twyman, since both Stokes and Twyman were inducted into the Naismith Basketball Hall of Fame based on their athletic prowess.

Jack Twyman was a slender swingman who was especially talented at shooting the ball. He finished his career as the University of Cincinnati's all-time leading scorer before spending twelve years in the NBA. During the 1960 season—two years after becoming Stokes' legal guardian—Twyman averaged 31.2 points per game, making him the first player in NBA history to average over 30 points for an entire season. However, that accomplishment is often forgotten because it occurred during the same season that a young Philadelphia Warriors rookie by the name of Wilt Chamberlain happened to average 37.6 points per game.

Despite all he accomplished on the basketball court, Twyman is most remembered for what he did off the court. He's remembered for his loyalty to his teammate and his ability to *get along*. Those who knew him best are quick to bring up his rare humility and his unassuming nature.

In a 2008 *New York Post* article, Jack Twyman explained his reasoning for helping his paralyzed teammate. "Maurice was on his own," Twyman said. "Something had to be done and someone had to do it. I was the only one there so I became that someone."

Saint Francis University, Stokes' alma mater, turned Twyman's quote into their athletic department's theme. Banners adorn the campus, encouraging students to reach out to those in need of friendship and brotherhood and to *Become that Someone.*

Shortly before Twyman's death in 2012, his grandson made him a get-well card. In it, Robbie Twyman listed The Top Five Things Grandpa Taught Me:

1. If you know it's right, don't worry about what others think.
2. Never quit.
3. Do the right thing.
4. Give it 100 percent.
5. Practice at whatever you choose to do.

Loyalty is the most sought-after quality in any relationship. Young Twyman's list captures precisely what good teammates do to authenticate their loyal behavior. His list is also an example of how to pass on *good teammateness.*

INVESTED

Ask a successful person if he or she had a favorite teacher growing up, and that person will answer with an enthusiastic, "Yes!" Ask the same person why he or she was so fond of that teacher, and the response will inevitably detail how that teacher "took an interest" in the person's life.

Having someone in our corner—someone who takes an interest in us, and in so doing raises our confidence and inspires us to want to be better—is comforting. As the adage goes: *People will forget what you said; people will forget what you did; but people will never forget how you made them feel.*

Good teachers have a knack for making their students feel special by taking an interest in them. They unlock their minds by touching their hearts. In studying the art of being a good teammate, I discovered that unlocking minds by touching hearts is what good teammates do. In fact, when I was searching for a label for this behavior, I initially called it "interested." But I realized that label was insufficient. Good teammates are more than just interested; they're *invested*. The distinction is subtle yet crucial.

When you are interested in people, you want to know more about them. You ask questions about the details of their lives. You want insight into their hopes and their dreams. You want to know what drives them.

On the surface, being interested suggests that you care about them. Dig a little deeper, however, and that caring may not be as true as it appeared. Individuals who are interested aren't in the *we gear* because the outcome doesn't matter to them. They wish others well, and genuinely hope things work out for the best. They may even be happy if all goes well, but that is the extent of their commitment.

Those who are invested, in addition to doing everything interested individuals do, care about the outcome. The end result matters. They are not just happy if things work out for the best; they attach their own success to what happens. Being invested means they see their teammates' failures as their failures, and they adopt an uncommon commitment to preventing and/or reversing those failures.

Good teammates want to know what they can do to help others become successful. Helping others is their way of expressing how much they care. The act of being invested is what allows good teammates to feel whole and enables them to experience fulfillment through helping others achieve higher levels of success.

Investment Lessons from the Financial World

We associate the word invest with the financial world. While investing in a business venture is different from investing in a teammate, we can learn about both kinds of investing from the practices of effective financiers.

Warren Buffett, perhaps the most influential investor in modern history, is known for frugality. Despite being a billionaire, he has lived in the same house that he bought in 1958 for $31,000. Some would say that his house is more of a statement about self-discipline in regard to simplicity than frugality. The real secret to Buffett's success is often accredited to the discipline he demonstrates in his decision-making. He is famously quoted as advising other investors: "Never invest in a business you cannot understand."

Consistently successful investors do their homework before they buy stock in a business. They want to know its leadership structure. They want to know its financial history. They want to know its projected earnings. They want to know how that business fits into the future of its industry, and what makes it work. Good investors go to great lengths to acquire these vital details. What they don't do is expect this information to be readily revealed. They understand that the responsibility to acquire this information is theirs. They strategically seek the answers they need by asking the necessary questions before they make their investment.

Good teammates follow this same practice. They make the effort to acquire important information about other team members. I am sometimes taken aback at the depth of information good teammates can recall about their fellow players. They remember the names of their teammates' extended family members. They know who in a teammate's family is battling an illness or struggling with a life issue. They know the names of their teammates' pets. They even know their teammates' favorite places to eat and their favorite articles of clothing. They seem to know every detail of their teammates' lives.

The ability to remember these things may seem like an unusual gift, but it's really not. Remembering is a skill that all of us have that is just more noticeable in good teammates. The ability comes from their investment. They remember the information because it is important to *them*.

We remember important personal information like our passwords, date of birth, and medical history. We remember because the information is important to us. Good teammates remember important details about others because they believe that what is important to their teammates should be important to them.

Good financial investors are also known for the length of time they hold onto their investments. They are most successful when they are committed for the long haul. Warren Buffett once described Berkshire Hathaway's favorite holding period as "forever." Good teammates enter into a relationship with the other members of their team with the same kind of commitment. Their *long haul* perspective leads them to put extra effort into nurturing the relationship and makes it easier for them to see the extra effort and the extra time as worth it.

When it comes to investments, another favorite *Buffett-ism* revolves around the virtue of patience. Buffett said, "No matter how great the talent or efforts, some things just take time. You can't produce a baby in one month by getting nine women pregnant." Financial wizards like Warren Buffett know there are no shortcuts; the process of making a good investment takes time, as does building a relationship with a teammate. If a player tries to fast-track the process, his efforts will come across as disingenuous, and the relationship won't last. A player's investment in a teammate must be genuine. The teammate needs to know the player really does care about the outcome. Otherwise, the player isn't shifting into the *we gear*.

Refueling the Raptor

In the months leading up to the war on ISIS, reports emerged of Iranian fighter jets attempting to shoot down unmanned American Predator drones over the Arabian Gulf. This prompted the Pentagon to order that American fighter jets escort future drone surveillance flights in the region.

At the 2013 Air Force Association's annual Air and Space Conference, United States Air Force Chief of Staff General Mark Welsh described a dramatic encounter between a pair of Iranian F-4s and an American F-22 Raptor piloted by Lieutenant Colonel Kevin "Showtime" Sutterfield. Welsh's account, one of the only publicly disclosed air-to-air encounters involving the F-22, offers a rare glimpse into the superiority of the plane that manufacturer Lockheed Martin calls "the world's most dominant fighter."

The encounter began when the Iranian F-4s approached the drone and acquired it on their radar. However, the F-22 is known for its remarkable stealth capabilities that allowed Sutterfield to fly undetected below the Iranian planes and check out their weapons load before emerging on their left wing and intercepting them. According to Welsh, Sutterfield then radioed the surprised Iranian pilots and said, "You really ought to go home." They graciously and immediately complied with his suggestion.

The F-22 Raptor was designed for air-to-air combat missions. While stories like this one involving Lieutenant Colonel Sutterfield hint at the fear the plane's mere presence causes its adversaries, many F-22 pilots ironically consider an operation apart from outside confrontation to be more nerve-racking—nighttime mid-air refueling.

Nighttime mid-air refueling is loaded with risk due to multiple variables. While flying at approximately 400 mph, the F-22 pilot must maneuver his plane into position and "park" just below a KC-135 Stratotanker, a large plane carrying as much as 200,000 pounds of highly flammable jet fuel. The KC-135 is commonly referred to as "a flying gas station," although its bulky structure has led some military insiders to call it the *Iron Maiden*.

Once the F-22 is in position, a boom operator in the back of the tanker extends a twenty-foot long telescoping pole into an opening twelve inches in diameter located on top of the F-22. Fuel is then pumped through the boom at the alarming rate of 1,000 gallons per minute—about a hundred times faster than most automobile fuel dispensers.

Navigating the planes is tricky as the operator moves the boom into the correct position and releases the fuel. The maneuver is further complicated by the possibility of air turbulence and night darkness. The procedure is tantamount to threading a needle while wearing a welder's mask and riding a galloping racehorse. Factor in the occasional necessity for the crew to maintain radio silence during the refueling operation, and you realize just how nerve-racking the procedure can be.

A considerable amount is at stake during the operation. Fighter jets are not cheap. At an estimated price tag of over

$400 million per aircraft, the F-22 costs more to build than most NFL stadiums. The technology used in F-22s is sensitive; even a minor boom error near the receptacle could potentially affect the plane's stealth capability. But of greatest concern are the lives at stake—the lives of the pilots and of everyone onboard both planes, as well as the lives of their fellow servicemen and women and everyone else on the ground who would be impacted by a failed operation.

The midair refueling of the F-22 is an example of a situation where every member of the team must be invested in the operation. For this team, only one outcome is acceptable—a safe and successful refueling. The process demands the team's total investment.

When total investment is not expected, teammates don't feel bound to the *we gear*. They are more like independent contractors than teammates. Consider the sport of baseball. If a player comes up to the plate four times during the game and hits a homerun all four times and his team loses the game, people will not fault that player despite the failed outcome. They'll praise him for doing his part.

The same is true for the top salesperson of a company. The salesperson may be exceeding sales goals, even though the company is on the verge of financial failure. Outsiders would praise the salesperson the same as they do the baseball player who hit four homeruns because the salesperson is doing his or her part.

If the F-22 were to crash as a result of a failed refueling, would anyone involved in the operation be likely to receive praise for doing his or her part well? Should the tanker pilot make a piloting error that causes the tanker to contact the F-22, the boom operator will not receive credit for a job well done. Neither will the tanker pilot receive praise if the F-22 pilot maneuvers incorrectly and damages the boom. All of them must perform their component of the operation correctly for any member of the team to receive praise for a successful mission.

Good teammates view themselves the same as the members of the F-22 refueling team. They recognize that they must do their part and that they may not be able to control how well other team members perform. But they also recognize that their individual success does not supersede or even equate to team success—the only success that matters to them.

Because they know that their individual accomplishments alone will not make them good teammates, they go out of their way to accommodate the needs of other team members.

What Else Could They Have Done

Let's go back to the baseball player who hit four homeruns and the salesperson who exceeded sales goals. If they in fact did "their part," why aren't they thought of as being invested? We don't have enough information to make that determination without assuming that hitting the homeruns and exceeding personal sales goals was all they did. If this is the case, the more likely question is what *else* could they have done to be considered good teammates.

The baseball player could have gone back into the dugout and shared some insight he picked up while at bat. Maybe the player saw a flaw in the pitcher's delivery that gave away the kind of pitch that he was going to throw. Maybe he noticed the catcher sitting into position too early and revealing the pitcher's spot. Maybe the player could observe his teammates' batting and give them feedback on their technique.

The salesperson could share sales leads or effective deal-closing strategies with the rest of the sales team. Maybe she could take her colleagues with her on her next sales call and allow them to observe her technique.

Any of these actions could change the baseball player and the salesperson from merely being successful individuals to being invested teammates. To be both is possible.

The Beach Radio Thief

In the summer of 1972, psychologists conducted a study on the responsiveness of bystanders who witnessed the commission of a crime. Known as the "Beach Blanket Experiment," the study is often referenced and has been replicated many times in a variety of different settings over the years. However, regardless of the setting or the medium used, the results of the study remain consistent.

In the original 1972 experiment, psychologists staged the theft of a radio on Jones Beach, New York. They directed an actor to place his blanket beside an unknowing participant. The actor would then turn up the volume on his radio and recline for a few minutes before heading off to the boardwalk, leaving his radio unattended. Soon, another actor, posing as a thief, would swoop in and "steal" the radio.

Psychologists determined that participants were far more likely to confront the individual they believed to be stealing the radio if they had been asked by the actor to watch his belongings. That small request created an unexpected and strong emotional connection between the actor and the participant. The request led to the participant's becoming *invested* in the safeguarding of the radio. That investment produced compelling data.

Participants who were asked to watch the belongings intervened in the theft an amazing ninety-five percent of the time. Some of those interventions resulted in physical confrontations—a clear indication of the depth of the participants' investment. Comparatively, participants who were not asked to watch the actor's belongings intervened a mere twenty percent of the time.

The study was intended to provide insight into the likelihood of bystanders intervening in a crime they witnessed and under what conditions they would do so. That the experiment succeeded is safe to say. In many ways, the experiment restored faith in humanity while demonstrating how influential being invested in someone else is on the actions we take.

The participants' interventions were classic good teammate moves. When confronted with a clutch moment, they shifted into the *we gear* and acted. The emotional bond that came from the simple request to watch the radio led to an investment, which created loyalty, which led to action. In the context of being a good teammate, what challenges the team bonds the team. This maxim is as true today as it was when the beach blanket experiment was first conducted over forty years ago.

An Invested Gift

Tom Walter was hired as Wake Forest University's new baseball coach in the summer of 2009. He had spent the previous five years coaching at the University of New Orleans where he helped rebuild a program and a community ravaged by Hurricane Katrina. Kevin Jordan was one of Walter's first recruits after taking over the Wake Forest Demon Deacons program.

Signing Jordan, one of the top high school players in the country, was a big deal. He was runner-up in the inaugural Bo Jackson 5-Tool Championship and would eventually be drafted by the New York Yankees. Walter was ecstatic when Jordan opted instead to attend college and play for the Wake Forest Demon Deacons. However, the emergence of an unexpected illness during Jordan's high school senior season put that plan in jeopardy.

The illness initially stumped doctors. After a battery of tests and numerous doctors' appointments, Jordan was finally diagnosed with ANCA vasculitis—a type of autoimmune disorder that leads to kidney failure. Having lost thirty pounds, Jordan was unable to perform on the baseball diamond the way he had when he signed with Wake Forest the previous fall, and he wondered if Coach Walter would honor his scholarship offer. The coach assured him he would—the first indication of the extent of his investment in his new player.

Jordan spent the bulk of his first year of college strapped to a dialysis machine in his college dormitory. Frustrated, he watched his teammates take batting practice and snag fly balls—activities he loved but was now unable to do. He was taking thirty-five pills per day, and his kidneys were functioning at less than eight percent.

Without treatment, survival under these circumstances is measured in weeks to months. Jordan was in dire need of a kidney transplant. When none of his family members proved to be a viable match, he was placed on the National Organ Donor waiting list, with no guarantee as to how quickly a match might be found. He was told the average wait time was four to five years—an eternity for a college athlete who dreamed of returning to the playing field.

Around that time, Coach Walter volunteered to be tested to see if he was a match for Jordan. As it turned out, he was. Compatible organ donors are almost always family members. For a random person like Jordan's coach to be a match was miraculous.

So on the morning of February 11, 2011, Walter and Jordan were wheeled into operating rooms at Emory University Hospital in Atlanta, Georgia. The surgery resulted in a successful kidney transplant. Nearly a year to the date, Jordan donned a college baseball uniform and assumed his position in the Wake Forest outfield in the team's opening game of the 2012 season against New Mexico State. The day marked a triumphant return to a life Jordan treasured, compliments of his coach's generous, lifesaving gift.

To imagine a better example of a coach's investment in a player than that of Tom Walter and Kevin Jordan is difficult. Like Jack Twyman's assuming legal guardianship of Maurice Stokes, what Walter did for Jordan was a good teammate move of epic proportions. Twyman's move was derived from loyalty. Walter's was derived from investment.

Tom Walter's story is also a lesson in the significance of a leader's—in this case, the coach's—seeing himself as a member of the team, not an isolated, outside entity. Leaders _are_ part of the team, and they need to be good teammates, too. The most important label on any team isn't leader or coach or even star. It's *good teammate.*

Barriers to Being Invested

A leader's failure to see himself as part of the team is a result of several flawed perspectives that can prevent an individual from being invested in his teammates. Sometimes people choose not to invest because they are afraid they will get hurt or be embarrassed. They fear the possibility of being let down or that their coming up short would cause them unnecessary pain, so they deliberately maintain a "safe" distance from their teammates.

This way of thinking is *me gear* rationale. To avoid the possibility of being hurt or embarrassed might be what's best for you, but it's likely not best for your team. Sometimes being a good teammate means opening yourself up and being vulnerable to uncomfortable situations. One example is confronting toxicity on your team. Another is being loyal to an unpopular idea. Yet another is investing in something that may result in your getting hurt. Good teammates act despite their fear.

The flaw in the logic of not investing to avoid getting hurt is that individuals don't realize they are already hurting—the pain just hasn't surfaced yet. The *me gear* keeps them from reaching their full potential. The *me gear* confines them and doesn't allow them to be the impactful version of themselves that they could be if they invested themselves in others. When people finally understand this reality, they experience the pain of regret.

Ignorance is bliss until we realize that, in fact, ignorance is ignorance. The realization stings.

Circling

An individual's approach to time can be another barrier to being invested. Some people can't seem to afford the time to invest in another person. But good teammates find the time. How? They sacrifice their own leisure time—or at least it appears like a sacrifice.

My observations of good teammates have shown that this demographic doesn't necessarily see making time as a sacrifice because their happiness comes from helping others. The "sacrifice" for them is sharing, a means of helping. What could be more appealing than to spend leisure time doing something that makes you happy?

We have an issue in my home when it comes to investing and the matter of time. I have become acutely aware of how finite time is, and so has my wife. When it's gone, it's gone. As we grow older, time seems to pass faster and faster. Our perception of time causes us to try and maximize the precious amount we have by not wasting it. Unfortunately, this approach has led to *circling*.

Circling is an undesired by-product of being overcommitted to maximizing one's time or an unintended result of having too much respect for time. I'm the type of person who tends to bend over to tie my shoe and think *What else can I do while I'm down here?* Although thinking like this would seem to lend itself to ultra-efficiency and the ability to maximize my time, often such thoughts cause me to become inefficient and waste time.

As a society, we have become accustomed to filling the static gaps in our lives. We feel a need to be constantly engaged in activity. We have fooled ourselves into mistaking activity for action. Smart phones have contributed to this practice. For example, if we're standing in line at the grocery store, we pull out our phones and check Facebook. If we are in the doctor's office waiting to be seen, we jump on our phones and read the latest headlines. Sad to say, some of us consult our phones while we're driving and stopped at traffic lights.

Circling is one of the ways we try to fill the gaps. The circling scenario in my home typically goes like this:

I'll be working in my home office and my wife will duck her head in and say, "Are you ready to go to dinner?"

I respond, "Sure, let me finish typing this last email and I'll be right there."

As I continue to type, she doesn't want to "waste" time waiting for me, so she goes and puts a load of laundry in the washing machine.

I finish typing my email and see her doing laundry, so I start picking up our kids' toys.

She finishes loading the washing machine, but now she sees me picking up toys. So she starts to fold the laundry that was in the dryer.

I finish picking up toys and discover she's busy folding laundry. I don't want to interrupt, so I go back to my computer and start working on something else.

She notices me in my office and sees me back at the computer, so she starts running the vacuum cleaner.

This cycle continues until one of us eventually yells at the other, "Stop circling!"

Our attempts to fill the static gaps and our desire to not experience any dead space in our lives causes us to become inept in managing our time. Circling prevents us from being invested in others. Getting caught up in the particulars of our lives makes it easy for us to forget to make time to invest in the lives of our teammates, which can lead to regret.

The Curious Custodian

Not long ago, I encountered someone who demonstrated how heavy regret can be. This incident touched my soul and resulted in an experience too emotionally moving to forget.

I was speaking at an event when a custodian working at the venue caught my attention. He was mopping the floor in the hallway off to my side. The door leading into the hallway had been left open. The audience couldn't see the open door or the custodian from where they were sitting, but I could see him plainly from my position on stage. I am not sure why, but the custodian distracted me.

I became so fixated on his incessant mopping that I started to lose my train of thought—not good for someone speaking to a live audience. All I could think was, "Why does he have to mop right there? Why does he have to mop right now? And doesn't he know he's distracting me?"

The custodian eventually stopped mopping. But then he stood in the hallway, leaning against his mop, staring at me. Although he was standing in silence, he still distracted me. I decided enough was enough, so I shot him a quick glance, and we made eye contact. I assumed he had gotten the message that he should move on because he dropped his head and went back to mopping. He disappeared down the hallway out of my sight.

Soon he reappeared. Only this time he wasn't in the hallway. He was inside the room, with his mop, in the back of the audience. I wondered in frustration, "What is this guy's problem?" His presence had become something that I couldn't seem to let go. No matter where I looked in the room, my eyes kept coming back to him.

After several minutes of standing in the back of the room, the custodian moved forward and sat in one of the empty seats. Then for the first time, it occurred to me that he wasn't trying to distract me and that he wasn't up to anything peculiar. He was just listening to me speak.

This revelation calmed my mind and allowed me to focus on my speech. However, before long the custodian again caught my attention. Tears were rolling down his face. Something I said struck a chord with him.

Again I wondered what his problem was, but I wasn't annoyed. I was concerned. Because I didn't want to call unnecessary attention to him, I carried on with the presentation. When I finished, I remained behind to mingle with the attendees, which is one of my favorite parts of these talks. I enjoy meeting new people and hearing their stories, and from these exchanges I get ideas for topics for my blog.

The custodian lingered nearby. I could tell he wanted to say something to me but, for whatever reason, was reluctant to approach me. So I went over to him and introduced myself.

With his eyes again welling up with tears, he told me how much he appreciated what I said about being a good teammate. He said that his twelve-year old son had been repeatedly bullied at school. He and his wife had tried to stop the bullying by reaching out to the parents of those who were picking on their son. They went to the school and met with the counselor and the principal. When none of these approaches worked, they withdrew their son from the school. Unfortunately, this didn't solve the problem, either. The same youngsters continued to haunt their son online through cyberbullying. One day the father came home from work to find his son had taken his own life.

He told me that what I said about good teammates being invested was what originally drew him in because the idea resonated with him. His story brought a lump to my throat, and as I searched for the appropriate response, the man said something that I will forever remember: "All my son needed was one good teammate. One good teammate could have changed everything."

Those powerful words were an important reminder of the impact a good teammate can have on someone else's life. We never know how much others are hurting, or how close they are to their breaking point. A good teammate move—a compliment, a kind gesture, or even a high five—makes a big difference in someone else's life.

Actually, a good teammate move could make more than just a *big* difference; it could make *all* the difference.

As we continued to talk, I realized how deeply the custodian was hurting. He was filled with regret. Although he had listened to his son and tried to help him, he felt that he hadn't been invested in the problem, that he had never saw his son's problems as his problems until it was too late.

The notion that *one good teammate* can make a difference is a powerful and true belief as evidenced by the countless movements that have happened throughout history as a result of one person's actions: Mahatma Gandhi, Martin Luther King, Jr., Nelson Mandela, Mother Teresa, etc. In many instances, the *difference* that one good teammate makes is that of getting others to join the effort—inspiring others to also take action.

Your investment in a teammate might not move mountains, but it may inspire others to.

VIRAL

That good teammates inspire others to take action is a proven phenomenon. For example, a simple birthday indulgence changed Candace Payne's life. When the 37-year old from Grand Prairie, Texas entered Kohl's department store on the morning of May 19, 2016, I doubt she envisioned the extent of the change that awaited her.

Payne had stopped by Kohl's that morning to return some clothes and to purchase a new pair of yoga pants. After setting out in search of yoga pants, an item on the clearance rack—a Star Wars toy—caught her eye.

Normally, this cash-strapped mother of two could not justify spending money on something so trivial and impulsive. But it happened to be her birthday, the toy happened to be marked down considerably from its original price, and she happened to be a huge Star Wars fan. The combination of circumstances was perfect for her to give herself permission to make the purchase. Buying that toy turned out to be a good decision.

While sitting in her car in the parking lot, she decided to place her phone on her car's dash and film a Facebook Live video of herself opening the toy—which she made clear to viewers was for her personal enjoyment and not that of her kids, even though she knew they would eventually confiscate it. The video included nearly four minutes of Payne laughing hysterically as she donned her newly purchased talking Chewbacca mask. Her video went viral.

While you may not recognize the name Candace Payne, you may have heard of the "Chewbacca Mom" video that became the most watched video in Facebook history. Candace's video received more than 43 million views within the first 24 hours of being posted, shattering the social network's previous record. To date, it has been watched more than 177 million times.

Why the Wookie Video Went Viral

Payne was invited to visit Facebook's corporate headquarters. She appeared on talk shows, including *Good Morning America*, *Entertainment Tonight*, and *The Late Late Show with James Corden*. She got to meet J.J. Abrams, the director of the latest films in the Star Wars franchise, and she toured the mysterious Lucasfilm headquarters. Hasbro, the Chewbacca mask manufacturer, created an action figure in her likeness that says phrases from her viral video. And most recently, she authored a book titled *Laugh It Up*.

Of all the videos posted on social media, why did this video go the most viral? Payne's video didn't contain any deep, philosophical message. It didn't show any amazing feats. And it didn't feature any emotional images that tugged at viewers' heartstrings.

I have watched the "Chewbacca Mom" video dozens of times, and, like many others, I find myself unable to resist laughing along with Payne. I have also shared the video with audiences who, like me, were unable to resist her infectious laughter—and therein lies the answer to why the video went viral.

Payne's video made us feel good inside by evoking a strong physiological response to that good feeling—laughter. Payne's unique, over-the-top laughter is such that we start to laugh at her laugh—not at what is making her laugh. The Chewbacca mask doesn't matter as much to us as the sight and sound of her laughter.

Lots of funny videos on the Internet make people laugh. However, their content is subjective to what viewers define as humorous. What is funny to one person isn't always funny to another. But laughter is universally funny, and it is highly contagious. To suppress our emotional response at hearing the sound of laughter is difficult.

In many ways, Payne's video is an example of the psychological wonder known as *emotional contagion* that occurs when our emotions trigger similar emotions and behaviors in others. Research has shown that we mimic the facial, vocal, and postural behaviors of those with whom we interact. If someone around us is grumpy, we become grumpy. If someone around us smiles, we smile. If someone around us appears tired, we feel tired. With "Chewbacca Mom," we automatically mimicked Payne's laughter because to do so made us feel good. We then felt compelled to share what we were feeling with others.

Good teammates exhibit a behavior that elicits a similar response from the other members of their team. Good teammates can influence the emotions and actions of their fellow teammates through their own emotions and actions, and they are conscious of their ability to do so. They pay attention to their moods and monitor their moods' effect on the rest of the team. They shift into the *we gear* when they enter a room by altering their mood to meet the emotional needs of the team at that given moment.

If the team is down, good teammates don't perpetuate their team's somberness. They don't project an unpleasant disposition through their words or their body language, even if they feel down. Good teammates are masters of their moods; their self-knowledge and self-control allow them to lift the spirits of others in the room.

The *How* is More Intriguing Than the *Why*

How did the "Chewbacca Mom" video become viral? Most social media posts, including videos, go viral after a popular social influencer like a celebrity or a politician promotes the post on his or her platform.

In a TEDYouth video, which has been viewed more than two million times, YouTube trends-manager Kevin Allocca refers to these social influencers as *tastemakers* and considers them to be vital to videos going viral.

Think of the famous Ice Bucket Challenge in which participants filmed themselves pouring a bucket of freezing cold water over their heads. The Ice Bucket Challenge became enormously popular in the summer of 2014, raising an estimated $115 million for research in ALS (amyotrophic lateral sclerosis or Lou Gehrig's disease). Who started the movement is debatable, but we know exactly when it went viral. Most experts believe the craze started when golfers began pouring ice water over their heads and nominated other golfers to do the same. Those declining to participate were required to donate to a charity of the challenger's choice, although many chose to both participate and donate.

Chris Kennedy, a golfer from Sarasota, Florida, nominated his wife's cousin Jeanette Senerchia, whose husband Anthony Senerchia was suffering from ALS. In his video, Kennedy gave Senerchia twenty-four hours either to comply or to donate $100 to The ALS Association. Kennedy's dare was the first time the Ice Bucket Challenge was tied to the disease. The bucket Jeanette Senerchia used in her response would eventually be displayed in the Smithsonian's National Museum of American History.

From Senerchia, the nomination process made its way to Pete Frates, a well-known former Boston College baseball player who also suffered from ALS. Frates challenged numerous friends and celebrities, including NFL stars Julian Edelman and Matt Ryan who responded and got other celebrities involved, and the Ice Bucket Challenge went viral.

As Kevin Allocca pointed out in his TEDYouth video, comparable beginnings can be found in other viral videos. Paul "Bear" Vasquez posted a video of a rare double rainbow near Yosemite National Park that went viral after talk show host Jimmy Kimmel mentioned it on Twitter. Rebecca Black's "Friday" video saw a spike in its views and went viral after comedian Daniel Tosh featured it on his television show

Tosh.0. But that isn't what happened with the "Chewbacca Mom" video.

Following a more traditional path, the "Chewbacca Mom" video spread the way viruses like the common cold or influenza spread—through one-to-one contact. Payne only had a few hundred friends following her on Facebook when she posted the video. They watched and shared the video with their friends, who in turn shared it with their friends, resulting in a definitive example of an exponential progression that doubled in size each time her video was shared. The video had gone viral before any celebrity caused a spike in its viewership.

Most viral videos, including "Double Rainbow" and "Friday," occur in a ratio of 1:1,000,000, with the 1,000,000 coming from the followers of social media influencers like Jimmy Kimmel or Daniel Tosh. This fact is important to note because the way the "Chewbacca Mom" video spread accurately explains the viral behavior of good teammates.

A Lexicon Hijacking

Viral has become a coveted state for online marketeers. Viral can lead to huge profits for businesses and can even launch careers—as evidenced by the "Chewbacca Mom" video. Going viral has muddied the distinction between famous and Internet famous by significantly extending the proverbial fifteen minutes of fame. As a consequence, the term *viral* has come to mean *popular.* But before pop culture hijacked the term, viral had a different primary meaning.

Viral is a derivative of the word virus as in *caused by a virus.* The Latin word virus means a "slimy liquid or poison" and was originally used to describe animal semen and venom. In the computer world, virus still has a negative meaning. However, in pop culture, viral enjoys a positive connotation.

If you go back to the early days of the Internet and the era of e-mail forwards, people didn't label humorous or inspirational content worming its way through inboxes as *viral*. They called it *sharable*. If an e-mail made you laugh or in some way touched your soul, you wanted to share it with others, so you forwarded it to your friends.

Popularity is not a defining characteristic of good teammates. Good teammates are not necessarily popular. In fact, some are downright unpopular e.g., when they confront a source of team toxicity or break up a clique. At those moments, they are not well-liked by everybody on the team.

While good teammates' actions may not be popular, their attitude is always shareable. Good teammates inspire us to want to "pay it forward," to share whatever it is that we got from them. Good teammate moves prompt others to want to share the behavior they observe in the same way that they previously felt obligated to share touching e-mails.

Killer George

Early in my career, I had a short-lived but memorable experience working in radio as an on-air personality. Most people associate talent in the radio industry with the station's on-air personalities. But insiders are quick to set the record straight.

The real talent lies in a station's sales staff. They sell the advertisements and keep the station financially afloat.

Without them, there is no station. Sales staff are the actual lifeblood of the industry.

At the station where I worked was a salesman named George. George was a balding man with a comfortable waistline and a thick, broom-like mustache. He was an exceptional salesman. He had an *everyman* vibe about him that put people at ease.

George would show up at work in the morning disheveled. He might have cream cheese on his shirt sleeve from the bagel he'd eaten for breakfast, or a spilled-coffee stain on his tie. His shoe and his pant leg might be wet because he had stepped in a puddle when getting out of his car. People could relate to George and his morning struggles.

But people would be wrong if they judged George's abilities as a salesman by his appearance because, when it came to selling advertisements, George killed it. He was, by far, the best salesman at the station. What made George so effective as a salesman is what makes a good teammate viral.

George was a person who others described as "willing to give you the shirt off his back." He'd do anything to help anyone. His down-to-earth nature made him easy to approach.

If I happened to see him in the office, I would ask, "How're you doing, George?"

Most people would reply with a standard *fine* or *good* or *not bad,* but George always seemed to have a more dramatic reply. He would say, "Well, I'm doing better now than I was an hour ago." George's reply would draw you in, and you would want to know more. You would want to know what happened to him an hour ago. Of course, when you inquired, he'd tell you an entertaining story. By the time he was done, you felt better about your life because his story was self-deprecating or because it was inspiring.

Like all successful salesmen, George was a good storyteller. He wasn't the type who people found annoying. He respected their time. He knew how to *get in* and *get out*. He didn't dawdle in the conversation, and he recognized when it was over.

George connected with others through his stories. People remembered his stories, and they remembered him. His stories were so memorable that people couldn't wait to share them with someone else. Over time, his stories became *their* stories.

I have observed the same interaction among good teammates. They connect with other team members and strengthen that connection through their stories. Their openness and willingness to share personal—and sometimes embarrassing—information is a way of shifting into the *we gear*.

Keeping embarrassing stories to themselves would preserve their pride and keep their otherwise flawless image intact. But revealing their vulnerabilities and sharing their stories is better for their team because their showing humility creates stronger bonds among teammates. Mutual experience may be the top bonding agent, but stories are a close second.

He Asked for It

George's affable nature and his knack for telling stories contributed to his success, but they weren't the only reasons he was a good salesman. George believed in one crucial action before he ended an exchange with a prospective client: He asked for the sale. Many salesmen will present a case for why the client should buy what they're selling. They explain the product or service in detail. They offer valid points. They may even lay out the possible repercussions if the client fails to make the purchase. But most salesmen don't ask clients, point-blank, if they will buy what they're selling. George always asked for the sale.

That simple question presented his clients with an opportunity to make a commitment. As discussed in previous chapters, commitment produces loyalty and investment. Commitment elicits action. Consider the beach blanket experiment from the last chapter. Most participants did not commit to watching the actor's radio until he asked them.

The Ice Bucket Challenge succeeded for a similar reason. In each video, the person being doused with ice water nominated three others to take the challenge. The person put pressure on the others by *asking for the sale*. The nomination was tantamount to asking, "Will you participate?"

Good teammates are salesmen and saleswomen. They are purveyors of hope, vision, and sometimes change. Good teammates are perpetually selling the other members of the team on the concept of shifting into the *we gear*—of putting the needs of the team ahead of their own. Success requires that they to ask for the sale.

If a member of the team is engaged in toxic behavior, the willingness to confront the individual—and ask for the sale— is what differentiates a good teammate from a disengaged teammate. Let's say you overhear someone on your team badmouthing another member of the team behind his back. You've learned by now that you have a responsibility to confront that individual's toxic behavior. In your confrontation, you can tell the person that what he is doing is wrong and that it needs to stop. You can explain why badmouthing is detrimental and give examples of the damage that could be done by what is being said and how it could divide the team. But this admonition may not be enough. You will improve the likelihood of changing the toxic behavior if you confront the individual by asking, "Will you stop doing this?"

Asking for the sale facilitates good-teammate behavior's becoming viral. To set a good example and wish that your teammates follow suit is rarely enough. On occasion you must explicitly ask teammates to do what is needed or to stop doing what isn't needed.

The Hawks' Nest Bench Mob

The Monmouth University men's basketball team opened their season on the road against perennial powerhouse UCLA. The contest was a "guarantee" game, meaning UCLA was paying the much smaller New Jersey school tens of thousands of dollars to come to Los Angeles to play the game on UCLA's home court. Monmouth was guaranteed to receive the money, regardless of the game's outcome.

Guarantee games are not unusual in college sports. They allow the bigger universities to secure more home games and for the smaller, less financially well-off schools to supplement their budgets. Most guarantee games end with the visiting team accepting its blowout loss and happily heading home with a large check.

But on the night of November 13, 2015, the Monmouth Hawks pulled off an unexpected 84-81 overtime win over

UCLA. They headed home with their guarantee check *and* an historic win. They also headed home with something else that night—a new standard for bench decorum.

Monmouth trailed by as many as thirteen points late in the second half before mounting an improbable comeback to send the game into overtime. During the comeback run, television cameras began focusing on the over-exuberant reactions of the Monmouth bench players. The producers would immediately cut to the Monmouth bench each time the Hawks hit a big shot.

One over-exuberant reaction was an impromptu mime of a bull charging a matador—with a sweaty bench towel serving as the matador's cape. While it may not have been politically correct, the television producers loved it.

Dan Pillari, a sophomore guard for Monmouth, noticed that the cameras were repeatedly focusing on him and the other bench players. He also noticed how their reactions seemed to energize the players on the court. After the game, Pillari and teammate Greg Noack met in Pillari's hotel room to devise a plan to take the team's bench celebrations to a new level.

Over the next several weeks, the bench players gathered on their own after practice to choreograph and rehearse future celebrations. Their antics targeted pop culture and various current events. They included a recreation of Michelangelo's Sistine Chapel ceiling and maneuvers such as the *human scissors*, the *defibrillator*, and the *big catch*—where players posed for a mimed photo while holding a teammate who was pretending to be a dead fish.

On a nationally televised Thanksgiving Day game, Monmouth upset Notre Dame. The date marked the first win in the school's history over an opponent ranked in the Top 25. The game was bittersweet for Pillari who grew up a huge Notre Dame fan who slept in a bed with Notre Dame pillows and Notre Dame blankets. But his conflicted feelings didn't last long.

The antics of the Monmouth Bench Mob caught the attention of the national media. Their sideline theatrics went viral and were soon copied by basketball teams around the world. They became the highlight of that year's college basketball season.

Contributing from the Bench

Competitive players don't like to be confined to the bench. By nature, they want to be on the court, playing in the game, which is also true in other team settings outside of sports. To accept a subordinate role is not easy.

Pillari and his Monmouth Bench cohorts are perfect examples of the kinds of teammates who embrace their roles on the team, become masters of those roles, and then use those roles to make significant contributions to the team's success.

When I interviewed Pillari for this book, he recounted the discussion he and Noack had had in the hotel room after their UCLA win. They were concerned that their bench celebrations might become a distraction to other team members—something they didn't want to happen. They wondered if what they planned to do might be selfish on their part and not in keeping with being supportive teammates.

Individuals in the *me gear* don't think this way. Those in the *me gear* who think the attention they are likely to receive will benefit them personally give the decision no further thought. Pillari's mindset was uncharacteristic of someone in his position.

The attention the Monmouth Bench was getting could have caused other team members to become jealous—and jealousy can bring the viral behavior of good teammates to a screeching halt. Rock bands have broken up because the band's guitarist became jealous of the attention the lead singer was getting. Companies have gone bankrupt because one partner became jealous of the attention another partner was getting.

Pillari and Noack's initial concerns were put to rest when starter Micah Seaborn told them he wanted to hit more three-pointers in the games so he could look over at the bench and see what they were going to do. Their antics motivated him. The other Monmouth players and coaches echoed Seaborn's sentiments.

Good teammates are excited by the success of other members of their team. For the Monmouth basketball team, the excitement flowed both ways. The bench players were excited for the players on the court. Their celebrations—though sometimes scripted—were genuine. Their happiness was sincere. Likewise, the main players who were getting court time were excited by the attention the bench players were receiving. Everybody on the team seemed to be buying into the common belief that when one team member succeeds, they all succeed. The only success that really mattered was *team* success.

What was fascinating about the Monmouth Bench was that it was comprised of teammates who wanted to contribute more to their team but were limited in their capacity to do so by their various circumstances: Some were redshirts and not permitted to play. Some were injured. Some were too inexperienced to have earned playing time. Regardless, they were all searching for an answer to the question *What else can I do to make an impact and help my team succeed?* The bench celebrations were their response. The celebrations allowed them to be more engaged in the game, and they energized the other players and the fans.

They were good teammates being viral.

Victory Cake

If you spend time on social media, you've at some point thought, "Every day is something day!" National Talk Like A Pirate Day. National Underwear Day. National Skip Rope Day. National Sneak Some Zucchini onto Your Neighbor's Porch Day. (Yes, that is a real thing!)

I shake my head and chuckle at most of the designations. But every now and then I'll come across a holiday in which I don't mind participating. Not long ago, I noticed National Cheesecake Day was trending on Twitter. I happen to really like cheesecake. Only in my house, we don't call it cheesecake. We refer to it as Victory Cake. Of course, behind the distinction is a story.

Years ago, an older, wiser basketball coach relayed how important celebrating your victories is—to make a deliberate effort to pause and enjoy the post-win moment before moving on to the next event. How people celebrate isn't as important as why they celebrate.

Winning is not easy. Achievement in general is not easy. Neither happens without sacrifice and significant effort—and usually a little luck. By celebrating victories, people are not just rewarding themselves, they're paying homage to the sacrifices made.

When I was coaching, celebrating victories came in the form of my indulging in the guilty pleasure of eating cheesecake. After my team won a game, I stopped on the way home for a slice of cheesecake. That became the only occasion when I allowed myself to eat cheesecake.

I never voiced this personal, unwritten policy to my family or anybody else. One day, out of the blue, my daughter asked, "Daddy, can I have a piece of that victory cake?" I knew exactly what she was talking about. Although I had never mentioned it to her, she had been watching, and she noted that her father always ate cheesecake after his team won. And thus the term victory cake was coined in our family.

The term victory cake has been used before. During World Wars I and II, British and American citizens baked cakes to celebrate troops returning home. The cakes, made from ingredients that weren't rationed for the war effort, were referred to as victory cakes and shared a similar purpose.

Our family has used cheesecake to celebrate more than just wins on the court. If my wife gets a promotion at work, we eat cheesecake. If my daughter aces her spelling test in school, we eat cheesecake. If her younger sister loses a tooth, forget about the Tooth Fairy; it's time for victory cake! (Sometimes, victories are relative to the celebrant!)

"Celebrate your victories" has proven to be among the best advice I was ever given. In our home, we take this advice seriously. "Celebrate your victories" has become a life-theme for our family.

At one time, I was concerned that celebrating our victories might be perceived as bragging. I feared some people might think I was trying to rub my good fortune in their faces. But I no longer feel that way. Victory cake bonded my family—my team. It became our thing. The experience allowed us to share in the enjoyment of each other's accomplishments and to appreciate the idea that when one of us wins, we all win— much the way the Monmouth Bench's celebrations allowed every member of that team to experience the thrill of one player's success.

The concept of victory cake is a creative way for leaders to get every member of the team excited for a teammate's success and to share in the moment. Jealousy can prevent some on the team from being happy when another member experiences individual achievement. For example, we see this situation in sports where one player receives an all-conference honor and his teammate feels snubbed. A similar scenario happens in the corporate world when an employee receives recognition and another employee feels slighted. Of course, the same scene happens in families.

Victory cake can come in forms other than cheesecake. The idea is to find a consistent way for every member of the team to rejoice and feel good about the success of any member of the team. The purpose is to enable the success to be viral, for the feeling of shared accomplishment to spread through the team.

Being Viral Means Sharing

If invested means caring, viral means sharing. When you're in the *we gear*, you share your energy, your positive emotions, your stories, your knowledge, and your enthusiasm for the team's success.

The difference between viral videos and viral teammates is probability. Over 300 hours of video is uploaded to YouTube every minute. Twenty percent of YouTube viewers leave after just ten seconds of clicking on a video. The probability of a video going viral is astronomically low. People have a better chance of being struck by lightning than of having a video they uploaded to YouTube go viral.

However, the probability of a good teammate's actions going viral is more similar to the common cold than to an Internet video. When someone on a team has a cold, chances are that someone else on the team will soon catch that cold. The more contact and connections among team members, the higher the probability of the cold's being contracted. Thus, good teammates cannot allow themselves to be discouraged from taking actions that will lead to virality.

Spreading positivity is one of the best actions teammates can take for their fellow teammates. Viral behavior increases team loyalty, investment, and activity, and it is the force that encourages others to shift their focus from *me* to *we*.

Until now, the *we gear* has been explained by asking oneself *What is best for my team?* when faced with clutch moments. Now we come to the fifth and final common behavior of good teammates, one that requires us to introduce a new question.

Good teammates are empathic. This means they ask *why* before they act. In the next chapter, we will discover what this question means and how empathy may be the most critical component in the art of being a good teammate.

EMPATHETIC

Sympathy and empathy are not the same. Too often we confuse these different terms, or worse, we try to lump them together.

Sympathy is feeling bad *for* someone else. Empathy is feeling what it is like *to be* someone else. Empathy is sharing an emotional state with another person. Empathy can lead to sympathy, but just as easily, empathy can lead to tough love and to the proverbial line drawn in the sand.

Engaging in the behaviors of being *Active, Loyal, Invested,* and *Viral* can make you a good person. But these four behaviors alone are not guaranteed to make you a good teammate, nor will they allow you to shift into the *we gear*. Why? Because you are part of a team. You must factor in how your thoughts and actions affect the other members of your team. Empathy allows you to consider and appreciate the ramifications of your decisions from your teammates' perspectives.

Good teammates have a unique ability to empathize and see things from their teammates' points of view. Being empathetic allows good teammates to accurately answer the question *What is best for my team?*

Tanner's Totes

When Tanner Smith was in fourth grade, he was given a writing assignment: Complete the sentence: *"If I had three wishes . . ."* In his childlike, grade-school penmanship, he detailed his three wishes: to own a golden retriever, to play professional basketball, and to make kids with cancer laugh.

His first two wishes were typical for someone his age. What boy doesn't want a new puppy or to grow up to be a pro athlete? But wanting to make kids with cancer laugh is not the sort of dream a nine-year old is typically willing to *waste* a wish on.

Tanner's parents were understandably moved by their son's answers, so they rewarded him with a new puppy the following Christmas. Wish Number One—check.

After a standout career as a three-year starter on the Clemson University men's basketball team, Tanner signed a contract to play professional basketball in Europe. He first played for *Landstede Zwolle* in the Netherlands before signing with *MHP RIESEN Ludwigsburg* in Germany's top tier *Basketball Bundesliga*. Wish Number Two—check. Somewhere between seeing Wish Number One and Wish Number Two come to fruition, Tanner was also—perhaps most triumphantly—able to see Wish Number Three become a reality.

118

Two years after writing his original three-wishes paper, Tanner completed another homework assignment in which he reiterated his unselfish desire to make kids with cancer laugh. This time, his parents decided to invest in their son's wish. They held a Halloween party and asked guests to bring toys. Their plan was to donate the toys to kids their son's age who were battling cancer at their local hospital.

A few days later, 12-year-old Tanner Smith pulled a red wagon loaded with tote bags full of toys into Children's Healthcare of Atlanta—the first delivery of what would become known as *Tanner's Totes*.

A decade and a half later, *Tanner's Totes* is recognized as a vibrant, fully-functioning, non-profit organization. The charity has distributed thousands of tote bags to cancer-stricken teens and pre-teens in children's hospitals across the United States. The bags include the kinds of items that make kids laugh and serve as a much-needed distraction from their unpleasant treatments.

Tanner's Totes is an example of a good teammate move initiated by an empathetic teammate.

Tanner could relate to how monotonous spending long hours in a hospital is for a kid because he spent most of his childhood hanging out in one. His father, Craig Smith, was diagnosed with Stage IV non-Hodgkin lymphoma when Tanner was three years old.

Although a bone marrow transplant eventually sent the cancer into remission, the transplant caused Craig to contract graft-versus-host disease—a condition that causes white blood cells to attack the patient's own body. The disease forced Craig to endure numerous extended stays in the hospital, with Tanner by his side.

The idea to package the toys Tanner collected in tote bags spurred from a comment his father made during one of those extended stays. Craig was constantly being moved around the hospital and commented that he wished he had a way to carry his belongings from room to room—a common problem for lots of patients undergoing long-term treatment. Tote bags were the ideal solution.

Tanner Smith recognized an opportunity to impact the lives of others in a positive way. His response was a remarkable good teammate move, and his willingness to shift into the *we gear* stemmed from his capacity to empathize. He could relate to what it felt like for a kid to be confined to a hospital room for prolonged periods.

However, to make a good teammate move derived from empathy, a person doesn't need direct knowledge of what it's like to be the afflicted teammate.

Empathy from the Fourth Wall

Jacquelyn Saunders wondered if getting her fifth-grade boys to stop fighting with each other was possible. She seemed to have tried everything, and nothing worked.

As a family crisis therapist in the Christina School District in Newark, Delaware, Saunders observed increased bullying and physical confrontations among the fifth-grade boys at her school. She had introduced them to anger management techniques and worked with them for weeks on impulse control, but despite her interventions, she couldn't get them to understand how their actions affected the other students at the school. The boys were unable to grasp the concept of putting themselves in the other person's position, which left her unable to teach them empathy.

Saunders' school was in a suburban neighborhood where a number of prosperous businesses had once operated until a change in the economy caused those businesses to leave. The area, now filled with low-income housing, faced all the socio-economic challenges that accompany poverty.

One afternoon, Saunders found herself curled up alone at home on her couch. She felt frustrated that she was failing her students in not being able to solve the issue with the fifth-grade boys.

Then, serendipity occurred. A series of *PassItOn.com* commercials repeated during a break from the television show she was watching. The commercials were moving, and they brought tears to her eyes. They also gave her an idea.

The *PassItOn.com* commercials were first launched in 2001 as part of a public service campaign sponsored by The Foundation for a Better Life. They contain uplifting messages to inspire viewers to adopt positive values in their lives and to share those values with others. In addition to television, the campaigns have appeared on radio, billboards, and the Internet. They end with the value they are promoting, followed by the tagline *Pass it on*.

A favorite *PassItOn.com* campaign of mine featured hockey legend Wayne Gretzky. The message was: "Nice guys do finish first. Class and grace . . . Pass it on."

The commercials that caught Saunders' attention were about bullying in the school cafeteria. She knew how much her fifth graders liked watching television and how much they valued screen time on their various devices. She was curious as to what kind of reaction they would have to watching the

PassItOn.com commercials. Could these commercials help her students learn empathy?

Saunders contacted the organization that produced the commercials. They graciously sent her a CD containing all of the posters and videos from their campaign. The next week, she gathered her group of at-risk students and showed them the videos. As she had hoped, the videos worked. The students began to empathize. In this instance, a picture *was* worth a thousand words.

The students' attraction to screen-time allowed her to remove the theoretical fourth wall from the equation. She was able to replicate through the videos what she had been unable to replicate through lectures, role playing, or any of the other strategies she had used to teach empathy.

The results were profound. The number of fighting incidents dropped, and bullying was drastically reduced. A noticeable change occurred in the boys' behavior. By showing them the videos and letting them view the issue from the perspective of a non-participant, she was able to engage them in empathetic discussions. She asked these questions:

- "What happened in the video?"
- "Why do you think they did that?"
- "What would you have done in that situation?"
- "What would happen to you if you reacted that way?"

Saunders appreciated how difficult it is for adolescent boys to empathize. She also understood how these particular boys' problematic home lives complicated their ability to empathize.

Saunders may not have been able to relate to her students' lives, but she could empathize. Her creative way of motivating them to shift into the *we gear* and to become empathetic was a good teammate move that came from her own capacity to empathize.

The Influence of *Why?*

The story of Jacquelyn Saunders and her fifth-grade boys demonstrates that empathy can be taught and learned. Her resolve not to give up on her students and to find a creative solution to their problem was in itself a good teammate move, but the action she took to teach them empathy made the difference.

Psychological studies show that both children and adults are capable of learning to be empathetic, and that empathy-training programs can be effective. Sports coaches incorporate comparable strategies when they experience role conflicts among players. For example, basketball coaches may have their post players and guards switch positions during a drill. The guards learn how frustrating battling for inside position is, and then not to have the ball passed to them. Conversely, the post players discover that passing the ball to a post player when a defender is pressuring them on the perimeter is not as easy as it appeared.

Saunders did what all good teammates do before they pass judgement; she asked *why:*

> *Why were the boys not responding to therapy?*
> *Why wouldn't they stop fighting?*

Why were they unable to understand how their actions affected other students?

The answers lay in the boys' inability to empathize. As fifth graders, they may have lacked the cognitive maturity to appreciate what it was like to be in the other person's position. Saunders' willingness to ask *why* influenced the type of good teammate move she made. Good teammates always ask *why* before they shift into the *we gear:*

Why is my teammate acting that way?
Why is my teammate making that choice?
Why is my teammate not onboard with the rest of us?

They don't ask *why* so they can decide *whether* they should shift; they ask *why* so they will know what to do *once* they shift.

Good teammates use empathy to get to the root of the problem because empathy leads to solutions, not temporary fixes. Good teammates are interested in curing the disease, not treating the symptoms. Their desire to cure the disease is what keeps them from being superficial and reinforces their inclination to be invested. Good teammates don't want to just manage the problem, they want to *solve* the problem.

Asking *why* allows them to uncover opportunities to make *sincere* good teammate moves that make a difference.

Peeling Back the Layers of *Why*

Reaching the root of a teammate's problem may take more than one round of asking *why*. For example, a team member habitually shows up late for her morning meeting. Asking *why* reveals that she oversleeps. Advising her to set an earlier alarm won't solve the problem. In fact, that oversimplified advice might anger her and damage the relationship. To reach her problem's root requires the peeling back of more layers.

Why does she oversleep? Because she goes to bed too late.

Why does she go to bed too late? Because she works a second job.

Why does she work a second job? Because she is saving money for a new house.

Why does she want a new house? Because she wants to move her family into a safer neighborhood.

Oversleeping for her morning meeting seemed selfish until we peeled back enough layers to see that her tardiness stemmed from an unselfish motive—caring about the safety of her family. Helping her accomplish that objective is the key to resolving her tardiness issue. We would never have discovered the root of the problem if we weren't committed to peeling back the layers of *why*.

The Reality of Embarrassment

Reality television influences our lives. Regardless of whether the programming is truly reality or not, it provides many with a glimpse into what life is like for others. At some point, reality television allowed us to move beyond the social taboo of being nosy and allowed us to snoop into the lives of *real* people—people who aren't actors *pretending* to be real people.

Watching actors portray real life has always been socially acceptable and never considered rude. But standing by and observing our neighbors—or even strangers—engage in the same behaviors would be considered extremely invasive. Reality television blurs those lines and circumvents the offensiveness of being emotionally engaged, uninvited, in the affairs of others.

Much like the fifth-grade boys from Jacquelyn Saunders' school, watching reality television has led many of us to become more empathetic. A study from the University of Bonn in Germany concluded that watching reality television stimulates parts of the brain that trigger higher levels of empathy and helps us to create a connection between empathy and *vicarious embarrassment.*

Vicarious embarrassment occurs when we feel embarrassed while observing the embarrassing action of another person. We cringe when we overhear a co-worker mistakenly congratulate a woman on being pregnant, only to discover that she's just overweight.

Vicarious embarrassment is different from general embarrassment in that it is not caused by our direct participation in an embarrassing act. We weren't the one who mistakenly congratulated the woman for being pregnant. We were just observers.

Vicarious embarrassment is also different from emotional contagion (see Chapter 5) because it is not shared emotion simultaneously felt by both people. Vicarious embarrassment can be experienced solely by the observer, while the person involved in the embarrassing act is unaware of being observed. For example, the boss is delivering a speech to his staff, while, unbeknownst to him, the fly on his pants is unzipped. If he knew his fly was down, he would most certainly feel embarrassed. When you notice that his fly is unzipped, you experience the embarrassment he would feel if he was aware.

The University of Bonn study shows that people with high levels of vicarious embarrassment tend to also experience high levels of empathy. Good teammates have elevated levels of both empathy and vicarious embarrassment. This combination compels them to subtly let a teammate know when his fly is unzipped, or when he has a piece of food stuck in his front teeth, or that he needs a mint. Most people would notice the unzipped fly, the food, or the bad breath but say nothing. Teambusters would discuss what they notice with others behind the person's back.

Vicarious embarrassment is the motivation for many of the good teammate moves that individuals in the *we gear* make, and it arises from their willingness to care. They treat their teammates the same way they would want to be treated if the situation were reversed.

The Montel Mantra

Looking at daytime talk shows of the early 1990s—arguably, the precursors to many of today's hit reality shows—we notice a correlation between their popularity and their hosts' ability to empathize with their guests and their audience.

One of the more popular talk shows from this era was *The Montel Williams Show*. Montel Williams, a retired marine, was able to differentiate his show from others in that genre by concentrating on inspirational stories like reuniting mothers with the children they had given up for adoption.

Williams won a Daytime Emmy for Outstanding Talk Show Host and was nominated for the same award on two subsequent occasions. He was gifted at getting his audience to empathize with the guests on his show. How? He focused on the reason behind his guests' issues.

In a 2017 segment of NBC's *Today* titled "Where are They Now: Talk Show Titans," Williams said, "Unequivocal, when you look back (at *The Montel Williams Show*), every one of the producers will tell you I had a moniker, and it was: We don't belabor what happens. We try to figure out why things happen and then we come up with the solutions."

Williams' "moniker" captures the approach good teammates take to confronting team problems. They don't dwell on the mistake; they focus on figuring out why it happened and what can be done to solve the problem.

Being empathetic doesn't mean you can't be judgmental. Rather, being empathetic means you *must* be judgmental— but try to understand the problem before forming your opinion. While you don't have to agree with your teammate's logic, you do need to be approachable, trustworthy, and receptive to hear and understand your teammate's views.

Our society is evolving such that people think they can't be judgmental. To appreciate diversity and to respect alternative ways of thinking is fine, but when you believe something is wrong, unjust, or otherwise disrupting your team's culture, you have an obligation to speak up and confront it. Failure to do so erodes your team's culture.

Part of the attraction we have to reality television comes from our craving validation for our life choices. We like to see our way of thinking authenticated in the actions of *real* people. We also like that our lives don't seem so bad compared to the train wreck happening on reality television. The danger occurs when we *enjoy* looking at the train wreck—without caring why the wreck occurred.

We can keep ourselves from falling into this trap by always considering the intent of our teammates' actions before passing judgment.

A Signing Blunder

From the perspective of teammates who made a mistake, having others consider the intent of our action and show us a little mercy is comforting and reassuring. Consideration and mercy can make us feel more connected to the person and strengthen our loyalty to him or her. I have experienced this kindness firsthand a few times.

A more humorous occasion occurred several years ago when a team I coached was scheduled to play Washington, D.C.'s Gallaudet University in a basketball tournament. I was looking forward to the game because I had tremendous respect for the players and coaches at Gallaudet.

Gallaudet is the world's leading educational institution for the deaf and hard of hearing. Make no mistake: athletes at Gallaudet are every bit as physically gifted and competitive as the athletes at any institution in the NCAA. Gallaudet's athletes just have an extra obstacle to work around. The creativity shown in how their coaches and players thwart the challenges of being deaf is fascinating.

The Gallaudet football team has been playing competitive football since 1893, making it one of America's oldest intercollegiate programs. According to legend, Gallaudet originated the football huddle. In a game sometime around the turn of the century, a Gallaudet quarterback suspected the opponent's defense was stealing the sign language plays he was calling, so he started gathering his team together in a huddle before each play. Soon every college football team copied the practice of huddling up between plays.

To overcome their inability to hear their quarterback call the snap count, Gallaudet's coaches used to beat a large drum on the sidelines. The players could feel the vibrations from the drum and used the beats as their cadence.

Gallaudet's basketball team integrated similar creativity into their repertoire. I had several conversations with their coach via a TTY telephone relay service during the weeks leading up to our game. He was kindhearted, and I developed a genuine fondness and respect for him as both a coach and a person. I decided I wanted to make our first face-to-face meeting special by greeting him in sign language.

I didn't know any sign language at the time, but I had a team manager, Heather, who was studying to be an American Sign Language Interpreter. Heather taught me a very simple greeting to sign to Gallaudet's coach: "Welcome! It's nice to meet you." We practiced the greeting numerous times in the days prior to the game.

When Gallaudet's coach and I finally met, we both smiled and shook hands. I then proceeded to sign the message I had rehearsed. His smile disappeared and his eyes grew big. I could tell by his changed expression that what I signed wasn't right.

I turned to Heather who was standing nearby clearly experiencing a moment of vicarious embarrassment, and my suspicions were confirmed. Instead of signing "Nice to meet you," I had signed "Nice to have sex with you."

Fortunately, Gallaudet's coach considered the intent of my action. "Thank you," he said, "but I don't think my wife will approve."

The coach's empathy allowed him to make a good teammate move and cover for the unintended awkwardness that resulted from my good teammate intention. Sometimes, those types of interactions can be the most important good teammate moves.

Mind Your PD-*EQs*

Emotional intelligence or emotional quotient (EQ), has gained considerable attention over the past several years as it relates to team dynamics. Some of the biggest and most influential companies in the world now include a mandatory assessment of a potential employee's EQ in their hiring process. Many professional sports teams do the same prior to signing a prospective player.

The Institute for Health and Human Potential defines emotional intelligence as the ability to "recognize, understand and manage our own emotions and recognize, understand and influence the emotions of others." The term was originally introduced in a 1990 research paper written by psychology professors John D. Mayer (University of New Hampshire) and Peter Salovey (Yale).

Some psychologists argue that an individual's EQ is more influential than IQ in determining success in life. Empathy is a factor that shapes our EQ—as does self-awareness, self-control, and our other various social skills. For good teammates, one element of their EQ stands out above the rest: *They are acutely aware of their own annoying habits and the negative impact those habits can have on other members of their team.* Being unaware of these habits prevents an individual from being a good teammate.

Good teammates acknowledge that they have annoying habits, e.g., small quirks like twirling their hair between their fingers, talking too loudly, smacking their lips when they eat, etc., and they intentionally try to refrain from doing them around their teammates.

A link exists between their awareness and their ability to empathize. Most individuals aren't aware that they have annoying habits that irritate others. If they are aware, the natural response is an attitude of, "Hey, that's just me. Accept me for who I am." That response would be acceptable for someone living an independent life whose actions don't affect anyone else.

But for people living a communal life—like those on a team—to justify annoying habits doesn't work. Those annoying habits disrupt the team's tranquility and over time impact the team's culture in an adverse way. They become an unnecessary barrier to synergy.

As a good teammate, you can and should try to be understanding and tolerant of others with annoying habits. However, you cannot and should not *expect* others to be tolerant of your annoying habits. While this philosophy seems like a double standard, it's one that good teammates embrace.

As I stated earlier in this book: *Good teammates try not to inconvenience their teammates, but they never mind being inconvenienced by something that is good for the team.* To be tolerant and show mercy to a teammate who exhibits annoying habits is good for the team—and a way to shift into the *we gear*. Tolerance can be a good teammate move.

The Escape Room Escapade

I am not a fan of teambuilding exercises. I put activities like constructing paper towers, tying your group up in human knots, and falling backward into the trusted arms of your teammates in the same category as diets. Anyone who has ever dealt with weight loss will tell you that diets don't work. Lifestyle changes work.

The problem with teambuilding exercises is that the temporary high from completing a group task—like losing a few pounds when you first start a diet—doesn't last. The feeling is fleeting if you don't commit to making a change in your way of thinking. The high doesn't last any longer than the weight lost from dieting if you revert to your former habits. Teambuilding activities don't create the sort of good teammate mindset that needs to be embedded in a good teammate's psyche.

However, I *do* advocate using escape rooms to improve teamwork and to cultivate a good teammate mindset. I have done numerous escape rooms and have become somewhat of an escape room addict.

The premise of an escape room is that you're locked in a room with a small group of people. Somewhere in the room, the operators of the game have hidden the key that unlocks the door. They provide a series of clues and puzzles participants need to decipher in order to find the hidden key. The participants are given a limited time (usually an hour) to find the key and *escape* the room—oh, and by the way, participants pay the operators a generous fee for the privilege of being subjected to this "torturous" activity.

I assure you, the experience is way more fun than it sounds. Every escape room has a theme. You might be locked in a nuclear fallout shelter with zombies bearing down on you or in the secret bunker of a terrorist with a bomb set to go off. The theme adds to the fun. I also like that escape rooms pair participants with strangers. I like to see how quickly a group of strangers can become good teammates—if they're collectively able to shift into the *we gear*.

My success rate for escaping the rooms is good but not perfect. I remember the first time my group failed to escape our room. The theme for the room was a secluded summer camp. Our group was locked in a cabin and had to escape before our ax-wielding captor returned—à la Jason from the *Friday the 13th* movies. As the clock approached the final minutes, we came upon the last puzzle of the room.

To get the key, one of us had to use a long metal pole with a hook on the end to retrieve a box containing the key from behind a wall. The challenge was that the person who held the pole couldn't see the box from where he stood. The puzzle required another player to get down on the floor and peer through a small window near the bottom of the wall. The person on the floor had to direct the person with the pole in how to maneuver the hook. I was the person holding the pole. The person on the floor guiding me in how to maneuver the hook was a woman I had never met before that day.

Our group had been functioning well as a team. We had successfully solved every puzzle heading into the last task. But this last task was especially hard. I could not get the hook on the box. I was getting frustrated, and so was the woman trying to give me instructions. I didn't feel like her instructions were effective—and she didn't think I was good at following them!

With the final seconds on our clock ticking down, the woman jumped up off the floor, grabbed the pole from my hands, saying, "Here, give me that! I'll do it!" She fared no better than I, and our time expired. Our ax-wielding captor returned, and we lost the game.

The escape room custom is to take a photo of the group when the game is finished. If the group escapes, they get to smile while holding a big sign boasting *We escaped!* If the group loses, they must pose holding a sign proclaiming their failure. They are subjected to the shame of knowing that photo will be posted on the escape room's social media pages for all the world to see. Although I was disappointed, the experience was an insight into the value of teammate empathy.

As our group meandered around the lobby, waiting for our photo to be taken, the woman who grabbed the pole from my hands approached me and apologized for her actions. "I am so sorry. I didn't realize how hard it was to hook the box, and I didn't realize you couldn't see the box from where you were standing."

That's empathy—and her apology was an appreciated good teammate move.

A Lesson Learned and Applied

Mistakes happen. When we are trying to expand the parameters or our comfort zone, we are bound to make mistakes. But good teammates learn from their mistakes and vow not to repeat the same mistakes.

A couple of months later, I found myself in a similar situation in another escape room. This time, we were locked in a bank vault, trying to decode a message that had been scrawled on the wall.

The puzzle required one person to read the letters from the message aloud, while another typed the letters on a keyboard on the opposite side of the room. I was the person reading the letters, while my teammate typed the message.

My frustrated teammate kept asking me to slow down and repeat what I was reading, and I was getting annoyed with her. I couldn't understand why she was taking so long to type the message as I read it. Although I repeated the letters louder and clearer, she was still struggling. I stopped, remembering the lesson I'd learned from the pole incident, and asked the typist, "Why do you keep needing me to repeat the letters?"

I listened to her explanation and understood. The escape room designers had changed the keys on the keyboard. The normal A-S-D-F keys weren't where they should have been. The rearranged letters required the typist to search for each letter. A single wrong stroke caused the decoding process to reset, and we had to start all over again. My willingness to ask *why* caused our frustration to dissipate and allowed us to focus on solving the puzzle.

Escape Rooms incorporate the opportunity to work on all five of the ALIVE behaviors. The clock forces the participants to act. If they hesitate, they run out of time. The puzzles require that participants be loyal because the team won't escape if participants undermine each other.

The entire premise of the activity forces participants to be invested. The only objective is for the entire team to successfully escape the room. No participant experiences a sense of achievement if the group doesn't escape.

The euphoria of decoding a message or solving a puzzle that leads the team closer to finding the key generates momentum and causes participants' enthusiasm to be contagious. They go viral. The confines of the room and the ticking clock also make participants aware of how their mood affects other players during the activity.

Of course—and as previously explained—the element of empathy is ever-present in every aspect of the game.

Escape rooms remind us that good teammates don't blame, shame, or complain. And they don't use their EQ to manipulate their fellow teammates into blaming, shaming, or complaining. Good teammates use their empathy to understand and to determine what is best for their team.

Project Aristotle Revisted

In Chapter 1, I referenced Google's *Project Aristotle* study, which attempted to discover what makes a team effective. Google's researchers spent several years examining 180 different "teams" that existed within their company.

Research from that project showed that psychological safety is critical in creating effective teams. Amy Edmondson, a Harvard Business School professor, explains the concept of psychological safety as "a shared belief held by members of a team that the team is safe for interpersonal risk-taking."

Being empathetic is the omnipotent behavior for good teammates because it creates psychological safety for the other members of the team. Your teammates don't hesitate to take action, behave loyally, become invested, or go viral with their enthusiasm because they know you will not embarrass, punish, or ostracize them for doing so.

Your empathy empowers your teammates to shift into the *we gear*.

LIFE IN THE WE GEAR

So, are you a good teammate? Are you ALIVE? Do you shift into the *we gear* when you come to clutch moments in your life? Do you consider what's best for your team? Life in the *we gear* isn't always easy but choosing to shift from *me* to *we* is always worth it.

In the beginning of this book, I recounted the story of DeAndre Jordan's frequent use of the word *we* in his post-game interview during the 2016 Rio Olympics. (He said *we* twelve times in less than a minute!) Two days after that notable interview, the United States defeated Serbia 96-66 to claim its third consecutive gold medal. When the game against Serbia ended, Rosalyn Gold-Onwude—the same sideline reporter who interviewed Jordan after the semifinal game—interviewed Jordan's teammate, Carmelo Anthony.

Like Jordan, Anthony had just finished playing in a game in which he, too, had accomplished a significant individual feat. Anthony had just become the first-ever American to win three gold medals in men's basketball. He had also finished the game as the United States Olympic men's national basketball team's all-time leading scorer.

But Anthony's post-game interview had a noticeably different vibe than Jordan's:

GOLD-ONWUDE: Why was this one special for you?

ANTHONY: I know this is the end. This is it for me. This is it for me. I committed to something... [Anthony's eyes well up with tears, and he pauses for twenty seconds to gather his emotions.] Sorry. I committed to this in '04. I've seen the worst, and I've seen the best. And I stuck with it. We stuck with it. And I'm here today—three gold medals later. I'm just...I'm excited for me but also for the other guys who've never experienced anything like this. Coach K. Myself. Jerry Colangelo and everybody else who's been a part of this situation and been a part of USAB for... since I've been here. I just want to say thank you for allowing me to be one of the leaders of [sic] not of just our team but of our country. Despite of [sic] everything that's going on right now in our country, we've got to be united. And I'm glad I did what I did. I stepped up to the challenge. But this is what it's about. And representing our country on the biggest stage that you can be on. America will be great again. I believe that. We've got a lot of work to do, but it's one step at a time. I'm glad we represented it in the fashion that we did.

If you're wondering, he used the words *I*, *me*, or *myself* nineteen times during his twenty-sentence response. In fairness, he did use the use the word *we* five times, and he made what seemed like a rather noble effort to use his platform to address a social issue that mattered to him. But his use of *me* was still disproportionate to his use of *we*. His response isn't in the *we gear* to the extent that DeAndre Jordan's response so clearly was.

My intent is not to bash Carmelo Anthony or to portray him as a bad guy. Carmelo Anthony's answer to the interviewer's question was typical of someone who had just accomplished an extraordinary individual feat—and Rosalyn Gold-Onwude had asked him, "Why was this one special for *you?*"

Then again, she opened her interview with Jordan with a similar question. The difference was that Anthony instinctively interpreted the *you* in her question as being second-person singular—as most people would. To him, *you* meant individual. Jordan, however, uncommonly chose to interpret the *you* as being second-person plural. To him, *you* meant the entire team.

Most people would reply the way Carmelo Anthony did. Most people don't think or speak in the *we gear*—and that's a problem. As a society, we've become too accepting of this unfortunate reality.

But it doesn't have to be that way.

No Magic Required

Seven-foot tall basketball players who are agile and coordinated are rare. Three-hundred-pound football players who can run fast are rare. Lefthanded pitchers who can throw an 85-mph curveball are rare. Good teammates who consistently do what is best for their team are also rare.

Good teammates are valuable treasures to any organization seeking success. You might say good teammates are the magical ingredient in every successful team. The great irony is that you don't have to be magical. No rare talent is required for being a good teammate.

You don't have to be tall to be a good teammate. You don't have to be fast to be a good teammate. Neither do you have to be strong, pretty, handsome, wealthy, or intelligent. You just have to be ALIVE.

When you walk down the hallway, can you be ACTIVE and bend over and pick up the candy wrapper? Can you *act* and pull out the metaphorical weed that is causing toxicity on your team?

Can you find your own version of the Disney picker?

Can you return stray shopping carts to the corral, even though you weren't the one who left them in the parking lot?

Can you be LOYAL without expecting it to be reciprocated? Can you embrace the idea that loyalty is not a two-way street?

Can you prioritize your teams the way Mama did on bowling night? Can you resist the appeal of cliques and saying *I told you so*?

Can you be so INVESTED that you see your teammates' failures as your failures?

Can you fight the temptation to *circle* and not get caught up in the minutiae of your own life?

Can you be somebody's *one good teammate*?

Can you become a master of your role on the team and be VIRAL with your enthusiasm like the basketball players from the Monmouth Bench Mob were?

Can you be EMPATHETIC and consider the intent of a colleague's actions before you chastise his sign language faux pas? Can you ask *why* before passing judgment on a fellow teammate?

I think you already know the answer to every one of those questions: Yes, you can!

In many ways, the ALIVE acronym provides a checklist for good teammate behavior. ALIVE provides an opportunity for you to assess the type of teammate you are and the type of teammate I hope you want to be. Ask yourself:

Do I do this? Am I doing that? What can I do better?

You will naturally be better at some areas of ALIVE than others. You may be more inclined to be loyal than to be active. You may be more inclined to be empathetic than to be viral. The goal is to become good at all five of the behaviors. Showing a deficiency in one area means you have to put greater effort into that behavior than you do the others.

But know that mastering all five behaviors is possible.

The Backseat Savior

Most of us have done things in our younger days of which we aren't especially proud. That's part of growing up and experiencing the misguidedness of youth. I am no exception. Shortly after getting my driver's license, some friends and I engaged in what the adult in me now considers as having been a very stupid "game."

We liked cars, so we tried to see how many car dealerships would let us take cars for a test drive. In hindsight, I am amazed at how frequently the dealerships allowed us to drive the cars off the lot without being accompanied by a salesman. To our surprise, all they usually asked for was a copy of our driver's license—which we were happy to provide.

Anytime we were able to take a car out without a salesman, it was game on! We pushed those cars to their limit. We tried to see how well they cornered and how fast they would go. If one of us pushed the speedometer to 100 mph, the others would try to top that mark the next time. I cringe when I think of how dangerous this game was and how stupid we naïve teenagers were. But that's not the point of this story.

The stakes grew higher the more cars we test drove. Eventually, the challenge evolved from how fast we could drive the cars to how expensive a car we could convince a dealership to let us test drive.

One day, I talked a salesman into allowing me to test drive an expensive BMW sports car. I still cannot believe he was brave enough—or perhaps, foolish enough—to let us take it off the lot. To his credit, he was at least smart enough to accompany us on the test drive.

Having the salesman sitting in the passenger seat took away from the excitement of our game, but I still thought for someone my age to get to drive a fancy foreign sports car was cool.

The car had a semi-automatic transmission that I had never seen before, sometimes referred to as a *clutchless manual transmission*, which meant that the transmission functioned as an automatic transmission—unless you engaged the manual option that required the driver to shift the gears manually. Semi-automatic transmissions are more common today than back then.

When I drove off the lot, the car was in automatic transmission mode. Along the route I stopped at a traffic light and unknowingly I activated the manual transmission. The light turned green, and as I started down the highway, I knew something was wrong. The car wasn't shifting into the higher gear. The engine revved, and I wasn't sure what to do.

From the backseat I heard my friend Richie say, "Shift."

Yes, I thought. *I need to shift, but how do I do that?* The salesman remained awkwardly quiet. I assumed he wasn't saying anything because he wanted to make the sale and didn't want to risk offending me by pointing out my ignorance.

The engine raced even louder, and with greater urgency Richie repeated, "*Shift.*" The tachometer was now well into the red, and I was panicking. I couldn't find the shifter lever to change the gears or the switch to put the car back into automatic mode.

"On the floor. The shifter is on the floor," Richie hissed. "*Shift!*"

At last I found the shifter lever and got the car back in automatic mode. I was embarrassed yet relieved. Without Richie, I would have blown the car's engine for sure.

The moral is that we don't always recognize the "clutch moments" in our lives, and we don't always know how to shift into the *we gear.* Sometimes, we need a Richie—a teammate who will relentlessly encourage us to *shift.*

A Doctor's Dilemma

The previous story teaches another lesson: you cannot stay in the *me gear* forever. If you don't shift your focus from *me* to *we*, you will eventually suffer the same fate as that car would have if my friend hadn't intervened. You will burn out, and your soul's engine will blow up.

Bitterness and resentment will overtake you. Selfishness will sink your *ships* (friend*ships*, partner*ships*, relation*ships*, champion*ships*, etc.) This book provides you with the tools you need to be a good teammate. Are you willing to use those tools to fix your *we gear* transmission or the broken transmissions of your teammates?

Or will you behave like the patient who goes to his doctor complaining about not feeling well? After giving the patient a physical exam and running a battery of tests, the doctor suggests lifestyle changes. He advises the patient to change his diet, lose some weight, and get more sleep. The doctor also prescribes a medication to lower his cholesterol and schedules an appointment to see the patient again in a few weeks.

During those weeks, the patient eats the same diet he's been eating, doesn't lose any weight, and continues to stay up watching television half the night. In addition, the patient doesn't take his medication consistently.

When the patient returns to the doctor's office for his follow-up appointment, he tells his doctor he still doesn't feel well. How does he expect the doctor to respond? He didn't follow the doctor's recommendations, so of course he doesn't feel any better!

If you keep allowing the selfishness of the *me gear* to dictate your lifestyle, you are no different than that patient. If your bad mood continues to affect the momentum of your team, you will be habitually plagued by the same problems. Good teammates don't allow their woes to contaminate their team's flow, and good teammates are good patients—they follow the prescribed recommendations.

The Extent of Your Reach

If you are a good teammate, congratulations! I hope what you have read in this book gives you validation. If you are still striving to become a good teammate, know that the possibility of change is within your grasp.

If you're dealing with an individual on your team who is a toxic teammate—a *teambuster*—then you know what you need to concentrate on to get that individual to be ALIVE.

Remember the truth in the adage: *If you really want to learn something, teach it.*

The best *good teammate move* you can make might be to teach someone else to shift into the *we gear*. In this quest, you will likely discover your own path to becoming a better teammate and to finding genuine purpose in your life.

In Chapter 2, I wrote about the three questions I ask my daughters when they come home from school every day:

1. *What did you eat for lunch?*
2. *Who did you play with at recess?*
3. *Did you make any good teammate moves today?*

Their answers to the third question move me emotionally because these answers are evidence of how the good teammate seed I planted in them is growing. With this book, I planted that same seed in you. Don't underestimate what this means.

In an inspirational commencement speech at the University of Texas at Austin, U.S. Naval Admiral William H. McRaven reminded graduates of the potential they have for impacting the lives of others. His remarks were spurred by the university's slogan: *What starts here changes the world.*

In the speech, Admiral McRaven described a path where, over the course of the next five generations, the graduates could change the lives of more people than twice the population of the United States—if each of them changed the lives of just ten people. The good teammate concept and the introduction of the *we gear* has the potential to significantly accelerate and extend the reach of that change.

I wrote *Be a Good Teammate* for elementary students. If an elementary school teacher has approximately twenty students in her class each year, over the course of her thirty-five year career, she will have the opportunity to plant the good teammate seed in the hearts and minds of 700 students.

Operating on the same premise that Admiral McRaven used in his speech, the average human will meet an estimated 10,000 people in a lifetime. Thus, if those 700 students share the good teammate message with just ten percent of the people they meet, the good teammate seed the teacher planted will make it into the hearts and minds of 700,000 people.

If those 700,000 people share the good teammate seed with just ten percent of the people with whom they meet, the good teammate message will reach 700,000,000 people—roughly ten percent of our planet's population. You will find similar scenarios exist no matter what line of work you are in or to what team you belong. So while I wrote *Be a Good Teammate* for elementary students, I wrote *The WE Gear* for *you*.

One good teammate shifting into the *we gear* can change the world.

Appendix

Transcript of NBC reporter Rosalyn Gold-Onwude's
Post-Game Interview with DeAndre Jordan
August 19, 2016
2016 Summer Olympics—Rio de Janeiro, Brazil
Men's Basketball Semi-Final Game
United States 82, Spain 76

ROSALYN GOLD-ONWUDE: Deandre, it's no secret, teams want to take you guys out of the flow...out of a rhythm. How were you able to find answers here today?

DeANDRE JORDAN: We're just able to fight through it. Clay got hot early. We needed a game like that from him. But then ultimately, we...we...we just got stops and we were able to execute our offense.

ROSALYN GOLD-ONWUDE: Defense is your thing. How much did this team need a burst of defensive energy?

DeANDRE JORDAN: We really needed it. We've seen it in spurts throughout the tournament. But, I feel like, tonight and the other night probably were our best defensive games of the tournament. And if we can keep getting better, then we'll put a full one together and win the championship.

ROSALYN GOLD-ONWUDE: You used the word spurts. As you head into the gold medal game, how do you get consistency—a full game—of great effort and focus?

DeANDRE JORDAN: It's a game seven. The last two have been game sevens. Guys know how important this is. We really want this really bad for us and our country. So, I feel like, on Sunday, we'll have a full forty minutes.

ROSALYN GOLD-ONWUDE: Thanks, Deandre. Congrats.

You may have noticed that DeAndre Jordan used the word "I" twice during the interview. However, it's worth noting that both times he used the word to unselfishly differentiate his opinion from the sentiments of the other team members, not to be perceived as speaking out of turn. Interesting. . .

Notes

INTRODUCTION

Men's basketball results, box scores, and statistics from the 2016 Olympics can be found at: http://www.fiba.basketball/olympics/2016/

All-time Olympic records for the sport of men's basketball can be found at https://www.usab.com/history/national-team-mens/us-mens-olympic-games-records.aspx.

Rosalyn Gold-Onwude's post-game interview with DeAndre Jordan took place on August 19, 2016 at Carioca Arena 1, Rio de Janeiro, Brazil. The game and interview aired on the NBC Sports Network.

Statistics about American drivers knowing how to drive standard transmissions is from Eric C. Evarts, "Why Are Manual Transmissions Disappearing?" *U.S. News and World Report,* September 27, 2016, https://cars.usnews.

com/cars-trucks/best-cars-blog/2016/09/why-are-manual-transmissions-disappearing.

The statistic about the percentage of cars with standard transmissions sold in the United States is from Charles Fleming, "The disappearing stick shift: Less than 3% of cars sold in the U.S. have manual transmissions." *The Los Angeles Times*, November 15, 2016, http://www.latimes.com/business/autos/laautoshow/la-fi-hy-disappearing-stick-shift-20161115-story.html.

Chapter 1
THE ME GEAR

Details about the Googles Project Aristotle were cited in Charles Duhigg, "What Google Learned from Its Quest to Build the Perfect Team," New York Times, February 25, 2016.

More information about Google's Project Aristotle study can be found at https://rework.withgoogle.com/print/guides/5721312655835136/.

Obituary of Anthony Swalligan was obtained from *Tribune Democrat* (Johnstown, PA), March 1, 2016, http://obituaries.tribdem.com/obituary/anthony-swalligan-1992-2016-751918971.

Additional details about Anthony Swalligan were obtained from an interview with Morgan Cypher (Anthony Swalligan's sister), July 19, 2018.

The op-ed piece about Anthony Swalligan was obtained from Chip Minemyer, "Mother Grieves for Son, Asks God to 'Damn Heroin,'" *Tribune Democrat* (Johnstown, PA), March 5, 2016.

Information about Chad Schilling was obtained from Eric Knopsnyder, "From Hero to Heroin," *Tribune Democrat* (Johnstown, PA), April 14, 2016.

Additional details about Chad Schilling were obtained from an interview with Pam Schilling (Chad Schilling's mother), July 20, 2018.

Information about the differences between pleasure and happiness were obtained from "The Hacking of the American Mind with Dr. Robert Lustig," September 8, 2017, *The UC Wellbeing Channel*, https://www.uctv.tv/shows/The-Hacking-of-the-American-Mind-with-Dr-Robert-Lustig-32572

The children's book referenced is by Coach Lance Loya, *Be a Good Teammate* (Cager Haus, 2015).

The Sports Illustrated article cited is Jake Fisher, "Oral History: Kendrick Perkins, the NBA's Best Teammate," *Sports Illustrated*, October 13, 2017, https://www.si.com/nba/2017/10/13/kendrick-perkins-oral-history-celtics-thunder-cavaliers.

Kendrick Perkins career statistics can be found at https://www.basketball-reference.com/players/p/perkike01.html.

Information about Kendrick Perkin's childhood is from Joe Gabriele, "Growing Up…Kendrick Perkins," Cavs.com, March 21, 2015, http://www.nba.com/cavaliers/news/features/growingup-perkins-150321.

Additional details were obtained from an interview with Kendrick Perkins, November 10, 2017

Statistics about stressful life events is from "The Top 5 Most Stressful Life Events," University Hospitals (blog), July 2, 2015, http://www.uhhospitals.org/myuhcare/health-and-wellness/better-living-health-articles/2015/july/the-top-5-most-stressful-life-events and "Top 5 Stressful Situations," HealthStatus, accessed November 4, 2017. https://www.healthstatus.com/health_blog/depression-stress-anxiety/top-5-stressful-situations/.

Details about the Dunning-Kruger effect are from David Dunning, "We Are All Confident Idiots," *Pacific Standard*, October 27, 2014, https://psmag.com/social-justice/
confident-idiots-92793.

The original Dunning-Kruger study can be found at https://www.ncbi.nlm.nih.gov/pubmed/10626367.

The original article about McArthur Wheeler—The Lemon Juice Bandit—is from Michael A. Fuoco, "Trial and Error," *Pittsburgh Post-Gazette*, March 21, 1996.

Details about PageRank is from Steven Levy, "Exclusive: How Google's Algorithm Rules the Web," *Wired*, February 22, 2010.

The BBC documentary explaining algorithms and PageRank referenced is *The Secret Rules of Modern Living: Algorithms*, directed by David Briggs (United Kingdom: BBC Four, 2015).

Chapter 2
ACTIVE

The Seth Godin quote about being remarkable can be found in Seth Godin, *Purple Cow* (New York: Portfolio, 2009), 124.

The Walt Disney quote about getting started is cited in Lewis Howes, "20 Lessons from Walt Disney on Entrepreneurship, Innovation and Chasing Your Dreams," *Forbes*, July 17, 2012.

Details about Disney Cast Members and being "onstage" is from Disney Institute, *Be Our Guest: Perfecting the Art of Customer Service* (New York: Disney Editions, 2001), 24.

The Disney practice of capitalizing Cast Member and Guest is cited in Lee Cockerell, *Creating Magic: 10 Common Sense Leadership Strategies from a Life at Disney* (New York: Crown Business, 2008), 2.

Stories and quotes about Walt Disney's rule of everyone picking up trash are from Van Arsdale France, *Window on Main Street: 35 Years of Creating Happiness at Disneyland Park* (Nashua, NH: Laughter Publications/Stabur Press, 1991), 74.

Additional information about Disney's training is from Doug Lipp, *Disney U: How Disney University Devolps the World's Most Engaged, Loyal, and Customer-Centric Employees* (New York: McGraw Hill, 2013), 155.

Chapter 3
LOYAL

Details about the Twyman-Stokes award are from Royce Young, "Billups Wins Inaugural Twyman-Stokes Teammate of the Year Award," CBS Sports, June 9, 2013, https://www.cbssports.com/nba/news/billups-wins-inaugural-twyman-stokes-teammate-of-the-year-award/.

Red Auerbach's quote about Maurice Stokes is from "The Legend of Maurice Stokes: One of the Greatest Stories in Sports History Unfolded Right Here," Saint Francis University, accessed April 15, 2019, https://sfuathletics.

com/sports/2012/7/17/GEN_0717123625.aspx?tab=maur icestokes.

The quote describing Maurice Stokes as the NBA's "first black star" is from Terry Puto, *Tall Tales: The Glory Years of the NBA in the Words of Men Who Played, Coached, and Built Pro Basketball* (New York: Simon & Schuster, 1992), 80.

Information about Maurice Stokes life is from Bryan Curtis, "The Stokes Game," *Grantland*, August 16, 2013, http://grantland.com/features/bryan-curtis-tragic-inspirational-story-maurice-stokes/.

Additional details about Jack Twyman is from David Whitley, "Remembering Jack Twyman, the greatest teammate in the history of the NBA," *Sporting News*, June 1, 2012, http://www.sportingnews.com/nba/news/292501 3-jack-twyman-maurice-stokes-foundation-tim-duncan-karl-malone-cincinnati-royals.

Information about the Foster Grandparents program is from "Foster Grandparents," Corporation for National & Community Service, accessed December 29, 2017, https://www.nationalservice.gov/programs/senior-corps/senior-corps-programs/fostergrandparents.

Additional details about the Foster Grandparents program can be found at "About Us—Our History," Your Aging and Disability Resource Center, accessed December 29, 2017, https://www.youragingresourcecenter.org/foster-grandparent-program-information.

The story about George Jenkins opening his first Publix store is cited in Brian Solomon, "The Wal-Mart Slayer: How Publix's People-First Culture Is Winning the Grocer War," *Forbes*, August 12, 2013, https://www.forbes.com/

sites/briansolomon/2013/07/24/the-wal-mart-slayer-how
-publixs-people-first-culture-is-winning-the-grocer-
war/#3ffd02a65880.

Statistics about Publix can be found at "Facts and Figures,"
Publix, accessed November 22, 2017, http://corporate.
publix.com/about-publix/company-overview/facts-figures.

Details about Publix and the other companies referenced in
the Fortune list can be found at "100 Best Companies to
Work For," *Fortune,* accessed April 15, 2019,
http://fortune.com/best-companies/.

Statistics about customer loyalty programs is from "U.S.
Customer Loyalty Program Memberships Top 3 Billion
for First Tme, 2015 COLLOQUY Census Shows,"
COLLOQUY, February 9, 2015, https://www.colloquy.
com/latest-news/2015-colloquy-loyalty-census/.

Details about Karam and Kartari's 90+ years of marriage were
found in Claire Wilde, "World's longest-married man
Karam Chand dies at age of 110," Telegraph & Argus,
September 30, 2016, http://www.thetelegraphandargus.
co.uk/news/14775553.World_s_longest_married_man_di
es_at_age_of_110/.

Additional details about Karam and Katari's marriage were
found in Sanjiv Buttoo, "Couple Karam and Kartari
Chand Married for 86 Years," BBC Asian Network,
January 7, 2012, https://www.bbc.com/news/uk-england-
16441633.

The BBC interview referencing the secret to the Chand's
marriage was that they never argued can found at
"Britain's longest married couple never argue," BBC
News, December 11, 2015, https://www.bbc.com/

news/av/uk-35068423/britain-s-longest-married-couple-never-argue.

Katari Chand's quote from the *Daily Mail* can be found at Keiligh Baker, "Now That's a Cause for Celebration! World's Oldest Married Couple with Combined Age of 211 Celebrate Their Birthdays on the Same Day," Daily Mail Online, November 24, 2014, http://www.dailymail.co.uk/news/article-2847871/World-s-oldest-couple-combined-age-211-share-birthday.html.

Statistics about Jack Twyman's basketball career are from John K. "Jack" Twyman, Basketball Hall of Fame, accessed November 24, 2017, http://www.hoophall.com/hall-of-famers/jack-twyman/.

Statistics about Wilt Chamberlain and Jack Twyman averaging over 30 points per game can be found at Isaiah Montoya, "NBA All-Time 30 Points per Game Players, Year-By-Year," Bleacher Report, https://www.bleacherreport.com/articles/414055-all-time-30-points-per-game-players-year-by-year.

Jack Twyman's "So I became that someone" quote was obtained from Peter Vescey, "When All Hoop Disappears," *The New York Post*, May 4, 2008.

Additional details about Maurice Stokes and Saint Francis University are from Valsilko, Rachel. *Believe, believe, believe.* Saint Francis Magazine. Sping/Summer, 2015.

Robby Twyman's list of "Top five things grandpa taught me" is from Pat Farabaugh, *An Unbreakable Bond: The Brotherhood of Maurice Stokes and Jack Twyman* (Haworth, NJ: St. Johann Press, 2014), 213.

Chapter 4
INVESTED

Information about the cost of Warren Buffett's house were cited in Nathaniel Lee, "Warren Buffett Lives in a Modest House That's Worth .001% of His Total Wealth — Here's What it Looks Like," Business Insider, December 4, 2017, http://www.businessinsider.com/warren-buffett-modest-home-bought-31500-looks-2017-6.

The three Warren Buffett quotes were from Paul A. Merriman, "The Genius of Warren Buffett in 23 Quotes," MarketWatch, August 19, 2015, https://www.marketwatch.com/story/the-genius-of-warren-buffett-in-23-quotes-2015-08-19.

The story about Lieutenant Kevin "Showtime" Sutterfield encounter with Iranian F-4s is from Eric Tegler, "Why the F-22 Raptor Is Such a Badass Plane," *Popular Mechanics*, June 14, 2016, https://www.popularmechanics.com/military/a21232/why-the-f-22-raptor-is-such-a-badass-plane/.

The Lockheed Martin quote referring to the F-22 as "the world's most dominant fighter" is from "F-22 Raptor: Modernizing to Deter and Defeat Emerging Threats," Lockheed Martin, accessed January 10, 2018, https://www.lockheedmartin.com/en-us/products/f-22.html.

Additional details about refueling the F-22 were obtained in an interview with Lieutenant Colonel Russell Badowski (F-22 pilot, United States Air Force), July 14, 2018.

An interesting read about refueling the F22 from the boom operator's perspective can be found at "Why Navy Pilots

Hate the KC-135," Fighter Sweep (blog), August 25, 2015, https://fightersweep.com/2881/why-navy-pilots-hate-the-kc-135/.

Statistics about the rate of refueling the F-22 are from "KC-135 Stratotanker," Air Warriors: Season 5: Episode 2, Smithsonian Channel, accessed July 14, 2018, https://www.smithsonianchannel.com/shows/air-warriors/kc-135--stratotanker/1003487/3437474.

Statistics about the rate of automobile fuel dispensers are from "Rules and Regulations" *Federal Register* 61, no. 124 (June 26, 1996): 33033-33039

Statistics about the costs of the F-22 are cited in Ralph Vartabedian and W.J. Hennigan, "F-22 Program Produces Few Planes, Soaring Costs," *Los Angeles Times*, June 16, 2013.

Statistics about the costs of NFL stadiums are cited in "Sports Money: 2017 NFL Valuations," Forbes, accessed July 1, 2018. http://www.forbes.com/nfl-valuations/list/#tab:over all.

A video of a midair refueling of the F-22 can be viewed at https://www.youtube.com/watch?v=wiZCMR6f0J0.

The story about replicating the "Beach Blanket Experiment" is from Eric M. Abschneider and Ann Varney, "Re-Creating the 'Beach Blanket Experiment,'" ABC News, March 16, 2009, https://abcnews.go.com/WhatWould YouDo/story?id=7091942&page=1.

The story about the original "Beach Blanket Experiment" is from Thomas Moriarty, "Crime, Commitment, and the Responsive Bystander: Two Experiments," Journal of Personality and Social Psychology, no. 31 (1975): 370-376.

The story about Tom Walter and Kevin Jordan is from Ryan McGee, "Coach Steps Up with Kidney Donation," *ESPN*, February 8, 2011, http://www.espn.com/college-sports/news/story?id=6100759.

Additional details about the Tom Walter and Kevin Jordan story were also obtained from Dan Collins, "Living Lives of Courage," *Winston-Salem Journal* (Winston-Salem, NC), February 10, 2011, https://www.journalnow.com/archives/living-lives-of-courage/article_4513734e-8ee5-5d49-aaf5-cb900ec5e1ae.html.

Additional details about the Tom Walter and Kevin Jordan story were obtained from an interview with Tom Walter, August 2, 2018.

Details about Kevin Jordan's participation in the Bo Jackson event were from Jim Ecker, "Bo Jackson 5-Tool Event Set for TV," Perfect Game, June 3, 2010, https://www.perfectgame.org/Articles/View.aspx?article=4814.

Career statistics for Kevin Jordan can be found at http://www.wakeforestsports.com/sports/m-basebl/mtt/jordan_kevin00.html.

Additional details about the Tom Walter and Kevin Jordan story are from *E:60*, Season 6, Episode 1, "Sacrifice," October 2, 2012, ESPN, https://www.youtube.com/watch?v=E8gKbK4yawc

Chapter 5
VIRAL

The story of Candace Payne's viral video was obtained from *Candace Payne, Laugh It Up: Experience Freedom and*

Defiant Joy (Grand Rapids, Michigan: Zondervan, 2017), 14-17.

Additional details about Candace Payne were obtained from Joel Comm, "18 Months After Viral Fame, Chewbacca Mom Pursues a Path of Inspiration," Inc, November 22, 2017, https://www.inc.com/joel-comm/chewbacca-mom -on-joy-authenticity-life-after-viral-fame.html.

Additional details about Candace Payne were obtained from "About Candace," Candace Payne, accessed March 7, 2018, https://candacepayne.me/about-candace-payne/.

The original Facebook "Chewbacca Mom" video from May 19, 2016 can be viewed at https://www.facebook.com/ candaceSpayne/videos/10209653193067040/?fref=mentio ns.

The definition of emotional contagion comes from Elaine Hatfield et al, "Emotional Contagion," *Sage Journals* 2, no. 3 (June 1, 1993): 96.

The TEDYouth video about "tastemakers" can be viewed at Kevin Allocca, "Why Videos Go Viral," TedYouth, November 15, 2001, https://www.ted.com/talks/ kevin_allocca_why_videos_go_viral.

Statistics about the "Ice Bucket Challenge" are from "ALS Challenge Commitments," ALS Association, accessed July 14, 2018, http://www.alsa.org/fight-als/ice-bucket-chall enge-spending.html.

The story about the origins of the "Ice Bucket Challege" are from Alexandra Sifferlin, "Here's How the ALS Ice Bucket Challenge Actually Started," *Time*, August 18, 2014, http://time.com/3136507/als-ice-bucket-challenge- started/.

Chris Kennedy's original Ice Bucket Challenge video can be view at https://www.youtube.com/watch?time_continue =18&v=WpJCWjs6kYA.

Details about Jeannette's Senerchia's bucket being placed in the Smithsonian Institute are from "Smithsonian Accepts ALS 'Ice Bucket' for Philanthropy Exhibition," Smithsonian, November 29, 2016, http://americanhistory. si.edu/press/releases/smithsonian-accepts-als-%E2%80%9Cice-bucket%E2%80%9D-philanthropy-exhibition.

The story about Peter Frates getting celebrities involved in the "Ice Bucket Challenge" is from JuJu Chang, John Kapetaneas, and Jasmine Brown, "How a Former Baseball Player's Fight Against ALS Led to the Ice Bucket Challenge Internet Sensation," ABC News, September 28, 2017, https://abcnews.go.com/Health/baseball-players-fight-als-ice-bucket-challenge-internet/story?id=50152750.

The definition of "virus" is from Robert M. Krug and Robert R. Wagner, "Virus," Encyclopedia Britannica, accessed February 28, 2018, https://www.britannica.com/science/virus.

The explanation for the origin of the word viral is from Dave Wilton, "Virus/Viral," Wordorigins, December 21, 2013, http://www.wordorigins.org/index.php/site/comments/virus_viral/.

Details about the Monmouth Bench Mob story are from an interview with Dan Pillari, February 23, 2018.

Details about the Monmouth/UCLA "guarantee" game are from Josh Newman, "Monmouth Stuns UCLA in overtime at Pauley Pavilion," Asbury Park Press (Asbury Park, NJ), November 15, 2014, https://www.app.com/

story/sports/college/monmouth-university/2015/11/14/
monmouth-stuns-ucla-overtime-pauley-pavilion/
75759042/.

For more information about "National Days" see "Calendar at a Glance," National Day Calendar, accessed July 27, 2017, https://nationaldaycalendar.com/august/.

The story about "victory cake" used during WWII is from Gary Allen, "U.S. Helps in Locating U.K. WWII Celebration Cake," Leite's Culinaria, April 9, 2012, https://leitesculinaria.com/10567/writings-wwii-celebrat ion-cake.html.

Statistics about the about of video uploaded to YouTube is from "YouTube Company Statistics," Statistic Brain Research Institute, September 1, 2016, https://www. statisticbrain.com/youtube-statistics/.

Statistics about how long people watch YouTube videos is from Salmon Aslam, "YouTube by the Numbers: Stats, Demographics, and Fun Facts," Omnicore (blog), February 5, 2018, https://www.omnicoreagency.com/ youtube-statistics/.

Chapter 6
EMPATHETIC

Information about Tanner's Totes is from "About Us," Tanner's Totes, accessed February 26, 2018, https://www.tannerstotes.com/about.

Additional details about Tanner's Totes were obtained from an interview with Tanner Smith, August 1, 2018.

NOTES

The story about Jacquelyn Saunders and her fifth-grade boys was obtained from an interview with Jacquelyn Saunders, February 28, 2018.

Information about the PassItOn.com commercials is from Stuart Elliot, "The Media Business: Advertising; A Campaign Promotes Noble Behavior and the Adoption of Better Values by Everyone," *New York Times*, November 8, 2001.

Wayne's Gretzky's *PassItOn.com* billboard can be found at https://www.passiton.com/inspirational-sayings-billboards/6-class-and-grace.

Information relating to the success of empathy training is from Emily Teding van Berkhout and John M. Malouff, "The Efficacy of Empathy Training: A Meta-Analysis of Randomized Controlled Trials," *Journal of Counseling Psychology* 63, no 1 (2016): 32-41.

The study about reality television leading people to be more empathetic can be found at Martin Melchers et al, "Reality TV and Vicarious Embarrassment: An fMRI Study," *NeroImage* 109 (April 1, 2015): 109-117.

Additional information about the University of Bonn study relating to vicarious embarrassment is from Laura Muller-Pinzler et al, "When Your Friends Make You Cringe: Social Closeness Modulates Vicarious Embarrassment-Related Neural Activity," *Social Cognitive and Affective Neuroscience* 11, no. 3 (March 1, 2016): 466-475, https://doi.org/10.1093/scan/nsv130.

Soren Krach et al, "Your Flaws Are my Pain: Linking Empathy to Vicarious Embarrassment," *PLoS One* 6, no. e18675 (April 13, 2011), https://doi.org/10.1371/journal.pone.0018675.

167

Information about the Montel Williams show is from Mark Harris, "The Montel Williams Show," *Entertainment Weekly*, August 30, 1991, http://ew.com/article/191/08/30/montel-williams-show/.

More information about the awards and nomination for Montel Williams can be found at "Montel Williams Show," IMDb, accessed March 3, 2018, https://www.imdb.com/title/tt0120992/awards.

The Montel Williams quote from *Today* is from Sheinelle Jones, *Today*, "Where Are They Now: Talk Show Titans, Montel Williams Looks Back at His Groundbreaking Talk Show," aired February 14, 2017, on NBC, https://www.today.com/video/montel-williams-looks-back-at-his-groundbreaking-talk-show-876868163925.

Information about Gallaudet University is from "Who We Are," Gallaudet, accessed May 20, 2018, https://www.gallaudet.edu/about/who-we-are.

The story about the Gallaudet football team is from Dave McKenna, "Beats Losing: Gallaudet Football Dumps Drum, Pounds the Opposition," *Washington City Paper* (Washington, D.C.), December 23, 2005, https://www.washingtoncitypaper.com/arts/theater/article/13032311/beats-losing.

Information about EQ is from "What is Emotional Intelligence," Institute of Health and Human Potential, accessed May 1, 2018, https://www.ihhp.com/meaning-of-emotional-intelligence.

Details about empathy factors and EQ is from Andrea Ovans, "How Emotional Intelligence Became a Key Leadership Skill," Harvard Business Review, APRIL 28, 2015,

https://hbr.org/2015/04/how-emotional-intelligence-be
came-a-key-leadership-skill.

The quote from Amy Edmondson about psychological safety
is from Amy Edmondson, "Psychological Safety and
Learning Behavior in Work Teams," *Administrative Science
Quarterly* 44, no. 2 (June 1999): 350.

Chapter 7
LIFE IN THE *WE* GEAR

Information about the USA men's basketball team winning
the gold medal at the Rio Olympics is from Sam Amick,
"Kevin Durant, USA Blow Out Serbia to Win Olympic
Gold," USA Today, August 21, 2016, https://www.
usatoday.com/story/sports/olympics/rio-
2016/2016/08/21/usa-defeats-serbia-gold-medal-game-
kevin-durant/89079370/.

Statistics about Carmelo Anthony are from "Carmelo
Anthony," USA Basketball, accessed April 22, 2017,
https://www.usab.com/basketball/players/mens/a/anthony
-carmelo.aspx

Rosalyn Gold-Onwude's post-game interview with Carmelo
Anthony took place on August 21, 2016 at Carioca Arena
1, Rio de Janeiro, Brazil. The game and interview aired on
the NBC Sports Network.

Admiral William H. McRaven's 2014 commencement speech
at the University of Texas at Austin can be viewed at
https://www.youtube.com/watch?v=pxBQLFLei70.

INDEX

Abrams, J.J., 100
active, 24, 35, 36, 37, 60, 117, 142
addiction, 13, 14
algorithms, 33, 156
ALIVE, 4, 23, 24, 25, 29, 35, 136, 139, 142, 143, 147
Allen, Ray, 16
Allocca, Kevin, 102, 103, 164n
ALS (Lou Gehrig's disease), 103, 164, 165
America. *See* United States
Anthony, Carmelo, 11, 12, 103, 139, 140, 141, 154n
attitude, 18, 29, 105, 132
Auerbach, Red, 62

backseat, 143, 145
backstage, 45
badmouth, 108-109
baseball, 85, 86, 87, 88, 89, 90, 103, 165n

basketball, 1, 11, 16, 17, 56, 62, 77, 109, 111, 112, 113, 118, 123, 129, 130, 140, 141, 143, 153n
Be a Good Teammate, 15, 148, 149
Beach Blanket Experiment, The, 87, 108
Berkshire Hathaway. *See* Buffett, Warren
Black, Rebecca, 103
blame, 23, 39, 44, 137
blogs, 20
Bonn, University of, 126, 127
bowling, 64, 65, 66, 142
Buffett, Warren, 81, 82, 161n

care, 7, 15, 21, 29, 38, 46, 51, 55, 62, 64, 80, 83, 127
cars
    automatic transmission, 3, 144, 145

broken transmission, 3, 13, 146

manual transmission, 3, 144, 145

Cast Members, 44, 45

Chamberlain, Wilt, 77

Chand, Karam, 76

Chand, Kartari, 76

charity, 62, 103, 119

cheesecake, 113, 114, 115

Chewbacca, 100, 101, 102, 104, 164n

Chuck E. Cheese, 65

church, 17

circling, 92, 93, 94

cliques, 69, 71

clutch moment, 4, 23, 37, 38, 54, 59, 66, 88

Colangelo, Jerry, 140

COLLOQUY, 75, 159n

comfort zone, 59, 60, 135

commitment, 4, 24, 32, 60, 63, 64, 66, 67, 72, 75, 80, 82, 108

complain, 38, 44, 137

Complaining, 53

confront, 47, 48, 49, 51, 54, 59, 87, 105, 108, 128

confronting, 49, 51, 53, 55, 91, 128

culture, 48, 49, 104, 105, 110, 128, 132, 159

Cumberland, Md., 19

cyberbullying, 96

Darnell the Mover, 18, 20, 21, 22, 23, 40

daughters, 15, 39, 40, 41, 42, 44, 55, 147

Disney, 44, 45, 65, 142, 157n

picker, 45, 46, 142

University, 45

Disney Guest, 45

Disney, Walt, 44, 45, 156n

doctor, 93, 146

domestic violence, 11

dopamine, 14

drama, 8, 48

du Sautoy, Marcus, 33

Dunning, David, 26, 27

Dunning-Kruger effect, 27, 30, 33, 35, 156n

Durant, Kevin, 16

Edelman, Julian, 103

Edmondson, Amy, 137, 169n

emotional contagion, 24, 101, 126

emotional intelligence, 131

emotional quotient (EQ), 131, 132, 137

empathetic, 24, 35, 60, 117-119, 122, 123, 126, 128, 137, 143

empathy, 116, 117, 120-121, 122, 123, 124, 126, 127, 131, 135, 137, 138

employee, 5, 8, 45, 58, 72, 73, 74, 115, 131

enthusiasm, 18, 20, 24, 57, 116, 137, 138, 143

escape room, 133, 13435, 136, 137

F-22 Raptor, 83, 84, 85, 86, 161n

Facebook, 93, 100, 104

Ferguson, Craig, 47

football, 11, 129, 141
Foster Grandparent Program, 68, 70
Fresh Prince of Bel-Air, The, 21
Friday the 13th, 134

Gallaudet University, 129, 130, 131
Gandhi, Mahatma, 97
Garnett, Kevin, 16, 18
generic, 9, 10, 41
Godin, Seth, 41, 156
Gold-Onwude, Rosalyn, 2, 139, 141, 151
good teammate moves, 39, 40, 41, 42, 43, 44, 46, 49, 54, 56, 57, 58, 59, 63, 88, 90, 96, 97, 105, 119, 120, 123, 124, 127, 131, 133, 135, 147
Google, 8, 33, 34, 137, 154n
grabber tool, 46
Gretzky, Wayne, 121
guilt, 26, 114
Hall of Fame (NBA), 77
Halloween, 119
happiness, 13, 14, 18, 92, 112
heroin, 11, 12, 13, 14, 18
humor, 27, 101, 105, 129

Ice Bucket Challenge, 102, 103, 108
imposter syndrome, 35
inconvenience, 22, 23, 40, 43, 77, 132
invested, 24, 35, 60, 79, 80, 85, 86-88, 91, 92, 94, 96, 97, 115, 117, 124, 137, 138, 142

James, LeBron, 16

jealousy, 48
Jedi mind trick, 53
Jenkins, George W., 71, 7,
Johnson, Magic, 62
Johnstown, Pa., 12
Jordan, DeAndre, 1, 2, 139, 140, 141, 151, 152
Jordan, Kevin, 89, 90

KC-135 Stratotanker, 84
Kennedy, Chris, 103, 165
Kimmel, Jimmy, 103, 104
King, Martin Luther, Jr., 97
Kruger, Justin, 26, 27

lacrosse, 28, 35
lemon juice bandit, 27
litter. *See* trash
Lockheed Martin, 83
Lou Gehrig's disease. *See* ALS
loyal, 24, 35, 60, 61, 74, 117, 142
loyalty, 63, 64, 67, 69, 70, 72, 74, 75, 76, 77, 78, 88, 90, 108, 116, 129, 142
Lustig, Dr. Robert, 13, 14

Magic Kingdom. *See* Disney
Mandela, Nelson, 97
Mayer, John D., 131
McRaven, Admiral William H., 148
mindset, 4, 17, 112, 133
Monmouth University, 109-112, 115, 143

National Association of Basketball (NBA), 1, 16, 17, 61, 62, 77

New Zealand, 16
Noack, Greg, 110, 111, 112

obituary, 11, 12
Olympics, 1, 139, 151, 153n
opioid epidemic, 11
overconfident, 28

PageRank, 33, 34
parent, 5, 39
PassItOn.com, 121, 122
Payne, Candace, 99, 100, 101, 104, 163n
Perkins, Kendrick, 16, 17, 23, 155n
philosophy, 18, 22, 132
Pierce, Paul, 16
Piggly Wiggly, 72
Pillari, Dan, 110, 111, 112, 165n
pleasure, 13, 14, 18, 114
Pluto, Terry, 62
positivity, 22, 116
practice, 78
pride, 18, 37, 38, 40, 59, 107
Project Aristotle, 8, 137, 154n
Publix, 71-74, 75

Rodriquez, Sergio, 1
Ryan, Matt, 103

sacrifice, xi, 92, 113
Saint Francis College/Univ., 62, 78
salesperson, 42, 72, 85, 86, 87, 105
Salovey, Peter, 131
Saunders, Jacquelyn, 120-124, 126

Schilling, Chad, 12, 155n
seeds, 148
self-actualization, 11
self-indulgence, 13
selfish, 7, 8, 10, 111, 125
selfishness, 7, 9, 146
self-preservation, 10, 64
Senerchia, Anthony, 103
Senerchia, Jeanette, 103
serotonin, 14
service, 18, 22, 68, 72-73, 75, 108, 121, 130
shame, 38, 135, 137
sharing, 15, 60, 92, 107, 115, 117
shopping cart, 43, 44, 142
sign language, 130, 143
Smith, Craig, 119
Smith, Tanner, 118-120, 166n
Smith, Will, 21
soccer, 34
social media, 47, 100, 102, 104, 113, 135
Spartanburg, Sc., 18
Sports Illustrated, 16
spouse, 5, 63
Star Wars, 99, 100
Stokes, Maurice, 61, 62, 63, 77, 78, 90, 157n, 158n
success, 5, 8, 9, 24, 70, 76, 80, 81, 86, 107, 111, 112, 115, 116, 131, 134, 142
successful, 16, 47, 70, 72, 79, 80, 81, 82, 85, 86, 87, 90, 107, 142
suicide, 96
Sutterfield, Lt. Col. Kevin, 83-
Swalligan, Anthony, 11, 12, 154
sympathy, 117

Tanner's Totes, 118, 119
teachers, 5, 66, 79, 148
teambusters, 8, 12, 15, 28, 33, 34, 41, 49, 51, 56
teamwork, 8, 9, 23, 64, 133
Teresa, Mother, 97
Tosh, Daniel, 103, 104
toxicity, 8, 47, 49, 51, 53, 55, 91, 105, 142
trash, 37, 39, 45, 47, 157
treasure, 18, 40
Twyman, Jack, 61, 62, 63, 77, 78, 90
Twyman, Robbie, 78
Twyman-Stokes Award, 61

UCLA, 109, 110, 111
understanding, 3, 12, 14, 15, 24, 26, 34, 132

United States, 1, 3, 68, 72, 83, 119, 139, 140, 148, 151

Vasquez, Paul "Bear", 103
vicarious embarrassment, 126 127, 130
victory cake, 114, 115
viral, 24, 35, 60, 99, 100, 104 115, 116, 117, 143
virus, 104

Wake Forest, 88, 89, 90
Walter, Tom, xii, 8889, 90, 163
Welsh, General Mark, 83
Westbrook, Russell, 16
Wheeler, McArthur, 27, 28
Williams, Montel, 127, 128

YouTube, 102, 116

BRING THE GOOD TEAMMATE MESSAGE TO YOUR TEAM

Are you interested in bringing the "Good Teammate" message to your event or implementing strategies to improve the quality of the teammates you have on your team? If so, contact Lance Loya at:

Phone: (814) 659-9605

E-mail: info@coachloya.com

Website: www.coachloya.com

Twitter: @coachlanceloya

Facebook: facebook.com/coachloya

Join the movement and sign up for Lance Loya's free weekly *Teammate Tuesday* blog at www.coachloya.com/blog.

*If you have enjoyed this book or it has inspired you in some way, we would love to hear from you! Be a good teammate and *share* your photos and stories with us through email or social media. We want to hear from you!

About the Author

Lance Loya is the CEO and founder of The Good Teammate Factory. He specializes in getting individuals to shift their focus from *me* to *we* and discover genuine purpose in their lives. Lance previously wrote the children's book *Be a Good Teammate* and the adult nonfiction titles *Building Good Teammates: The Story of My Mount Rushmore, a Coaching Epiphany, and That Nun*; *Teammate Tuesdays: A Year of Good Teammate Musings;* and *Teammate Tuesdays Volume II: Another Year of Good Teammate Musings.*

A college basketball coach turned author, blogger, and professional speaker, he is known for his enthusiastic personality and his passion for turning *teambusters* into good teammates. He has inspired readers and audiences around the globe through his books, keynotes, and seminars.

When not speaking or writing, he is a loyal husband to his high school sweetheart and a doting father to his two daughters—who, incidentally, were the impetus behind his heartwarming children's book.

Also By Lance Loya

Be a Good Teammate

An illustrated children's book that teaches the importance of teamwork and how to be a good teammate. Good teammates care, share, and listen. You don't have to play sports to be on a team. This book encourages kindness and counters bullying.

Building Good Teammates

The story of Lance Loya's discovery of an alternative approach to coaching players to be good teammates. Explore how his personal Mount Rushmore—the four men who had the biggest impact on his life—and a quirky nun influenced his coaching methodology.

Teammate Tuesdays

A compilation of the entire first year of Lance Loya's popular weekly blog of the same name. Each chapter examines a different aspect of being a good teammate. Gain insight and encouragement through a variety of "good teammate" observations.

Teammate Tuesdays Vol. II

A compilation of another entire year of Lance Loya's popular weekly blog of the same name. Includes *musings* ranging from touching "good teammate" stories to creative ideas for inspiring team members to become better teammates.

WWW.COACHLOYA.COM

Made in USA - North Chelmsford, MA
1087957_9781732550544
04.22.2020 2104